"Nolo's home page is worth bookmarking."

—WALL STREET JOURNAL

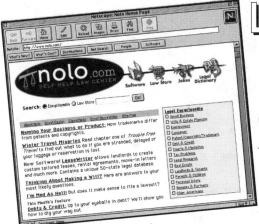

LEGAL INFORMATION ONLINE ANYTIME

24 hours a day

www.nolo.com

AT THE NOLO.COM SELF-HELP LAW CENTER ON THE WEB, YOU'LL FIND

- **Nolo's comprehensive Legal Encyclopedia, with links to other online resources**
- **SharkTalk: Everybody's Legal Dictionary**
- **Auntie Nolo—if you've got questions, Auntie's got answers**
- **Update information on Nolo books and software**
- **The Law Store—over 250 self-help legal products including:**
  Downloadable Software, Books, Form Kits and E-Guides
- **Discounts and other good deals, plus our hilarious Shark Talk game**
- **Our ever-popular lawyer jokes**
- **NoloBriefs.com, our monthly email newsletter**

Quality LAW BOOKS & SOFTWARE FOR NON-LAWYERS

Nolo.com legal books and software are consistently first-rate because:

- A dozen in-house Nolo legal editors, working with highly skilled authors, ensure that our products are accurate, up-to-date and easy to use.

- We know our books get better when we listen to what our customers tell us. (Yes, we really do want to hear from you—please fill out and return the card at the back of this book.)

- We are maniacal about updating every book and software program to keep up with changes in the law.

- Our commitment to a more democratic legal system informs all of our work.

OUR "NO-HASSLE" GUARANTEE

Return anything you buy directly from Nolo for any reason and we'll cheerfully refund your purchase price. No ifs, ands or buts.

AN IMPORTANT MESSAGE TO OUR READERS

This product provides information and general advice about the law. But laws and procedures change frequently, and they can be interpreted differently by different people. For specific advice geared to your specific situation, consult an expert. No book, software or other published material is a substitute for personalized advice from a knowledgable lawyer licensed to practice law in your state.

FIRST EDITION

Estate Planning Basics

**by attorney
Denis Clifford**

nolo.com
LAW FOR ALL

KEEPING UP-TO-DATE

To keep its books up to date, Nolo issues new printings and new editions periodically. New printings reflect minor legal changes and technical corrections. New editions contain major legal changes, major text additions or major reorganizations. To find out if a later printing or edition of any Nolo book is available, call Nolo at 510-549-1976 or check our website: www.nolo.com.

To stay current, follow the "Update" service at our website: www.nolo.com. In another effort to help you use Nolo's latest materials, we offer a 35% discount off the purchase of the new edition of your Nolo book when you turn in the cover of an earlier edition. (See the "Special Upgrade Offer" in the back of the book.) This book was last revised in: SEPTEMBER 1999.

FIRST EDITION	**September 1999**
PRODUCTION	Sarah Toll
EDITOR	Shae Irving
PROOFREADER	Robert Wells
INDEX	Sayre Van Young
PRINTING	Bertelsmann Industry Services
COVER	Toni Ihara

Clifford, Denis.
    Estate Planning Basics / by Denis Clifford.
        p. cm.
    Includes index.
    ISBN 0-87337-535-1
    1. Estate planning--United States--Popular works. I. Title.
    KF750.Z9C585 1999
    346.7305'2--dc21   99-21018
                            CIP

Dedication

To My Sisters and Brothers: Catherine, Justin, Douglas, Gregory, Steve and Joanne.

Acknowledgments

My thanks and gratitude to:

Shae Irving, for her perceptive and graceful editing, and for being so enjoyable to work with;

My other editors at Nolo: Jake Warner, Steve Elias and Mary Randolph for all their help over many years;

Stan Jacobsen, Nolo officemate and kindred spirit;

Toni Ihara for connecting me with Nolo, and her friendship for decades;

My other friends and colleagues at Nolo, who make it a free-spirited and unique place to write;

And, as ever, to Naomi.

CONTENTS

CHAPTER 4

WILLS

CHAPTER 5

LIVING TRUSTS

CHAPTER 6

OTHER PROBATE AVOIDANCE METHODS

CHAPTER 7

RETIREMENT PLANS AS ESTATE PLANNING DEVICES

CHAPTER 8

ESTATE TAX

CHAPTER 9

REDUCING FEDERAL ESTATE TAXES

CHAPTER 10

PROPERTY CONTROL TRUSTS

CHAPTER 11

PLANNING FOR INCAPACITY: MEDICAL CARE AND FINANCES

CHAPTER 12

LAWYERS

CHAPTER 13

FINALIZING YOUR ESTATE PLAN

INDEX

INTRODUCTION

Welcome to Estate Planning. Welcome? It may seem a curious word to apply to this subject, but I do mean it. Welcome, in the sense of being cordial, at ease. If you want to understand how to plan your estate, here you'll find a comfortable way to learn what you need. This book explains, in plain English, what most people need to know about estate planning.

"Estate planning" essentially means deciding who gets your property after you die, then choosing the wisest legal transfer method, or methods, for leaving your property to those you want to receive it. Your "plan," when completed, will simply be the documents necessary to carry out your basic decisions. Don't be mislead by the word "plan" into thinking you have to map out some grand strategy, like a military campaign, or that you must end up with a thick bundle of papers gorged with legalese. Many estate plans are quite simple and easy to create.

I won't pretend that estate planning is as stimulating as a good book or basketball or gardening or whatever piques your interest. But we all know we "should" think about estate planning, and then get it done. Here you'll learn that you can fathom the subject and grasp what you need. Over 20 years of practicing estate law and writing for Nolo have taught me that it is definitely possible for regular folks to understand estate planning and handle much or all of the necessary work themselves, if they want to.

The most important part of planning your estate is deciding who will get your property after you die, and, if you have minor children, who should care for them if you cannot. These are your personal decisions, certainly not matters for lawyers or other "experts." You can trust your own desires and feelings. Then there's the technical side; this book will give you the legal knowledge you need to confidently go ahead with preparing your estate plan.

DEFINITION: ESTATE

Your estate is the total value of all the property you own at your death, including any equity you have in a house. Value means the "net worth"—the market price of your property, less anything you owe on it, like a mortgage or other loan.

Underlying estate planning is a deep, understandable desire to pass property to loved ones. This book draws on my extensive experience with people's efforts to do this, from individual clients to Nolo readers to people who've attended seminars and classes I've taught. My experience affects this book in two important ways. First, the examples and problems discussed are adapted from real life. The lives reflected here are those of regular folks engaged in estate planning. Most estate planning books, written by professional estate planners for the wealthy, present only the somewhat skewed range of problems encountered by the affluent.

Second, I strongly believe that most readers of this book can handle their own estate planning problems, without a lawyer. This contrasts sharply with the attitude of many other estate planning books, which insist you follow what I call the "team of experts" approach. One recent book states that you must assemble "an estate planning lawyer, accountant, life insurance agent and financial planner (as well as perhaps a trust officer or stockbroker)." Perhaps a multimillionaire could benefit from such an expensive crew. For anyone else they certainly wouldn't be worth the cost.

Some readers will sensibly conclude that their situation does require the assistance of a lawyer. Indeed, you'll see that there are quite a number of instances where I recommend a lawyer's help. But even if you do need a lawyer, you should be able to understand the essentials of what she is talking about, ask intelligent questions, and be able to judge whether her fee is reasonable.

Finally, there are two things this book is not. It is not a book containing legal forms you can use to prepare specific estate planning documents. The purpose of this book is to explain what basic estate planning is all about, to demystify the problems and language involved so you'll be able to sensibly decide what forms you want. You can find a list of other estate planning resources from Nolo, including those you can use to prepare a specific form like a will or living trust, in Chapter 1, Section G.

Also, this is not a book on planning for retirement or old age. Although related, this major subject is separate from estate planning. Again, Nolo resources covering retirement issues are listed in Chapter 1, Section G.

To return to the positive, by using this book, you can figure out what you want to accomplish in your estate plan. For most people, once they know what they want, selecting and completing the necessary forms is not hard.

ICONS USED IN THIS BOOK

Throughout this book, the following icons will help you along.

 Circumstances when you may want to consult an attorney.

 Slow down and consider potential problems.

 Additional sources of information about the particular issue or topic discussed in the text.

 A bit of advice that may help you with a particular issue.

CHAPTER 1

A First Look at Estate Planning

Who needs to bother with estate planning? Here's the short answer:

- anyone who owns property that matters to them, and
- anyone with a minor child (under 18).

Estate planning isn't only for the rich, nor are there minimum property requirements, such as owning a home. Anything you care about—from art works to gold earrings to items with little or no market value such as the old family rocking chair or loved photographs—is significant enough to warrant at least basic estate planning.

The key is to ask yourself whether you own any property that you want to go to a specific person or organization when you die. If the answer is yes, you need to create a plan to make sure your desires will be carried out.

Example: *Tracy told me she had no reason to worry about estate planning; she was a carpenter. I asked her if she were sure she owned nothing she cared about. She answered "No, nothing—well, I guess my tools." When I pressed a bit, she estimated they were worth, in total, over $35,000. I told her that if she did no planning before she died, her tools would be divided, according to state law, between members of her family. She exclaimed that wasn't what she wanted at all. Everyone knew she wanted her tools to go to her partner, Alex. I explained that she could guarantee her goal by preparing a very simple will. Later, having prepared a will, she told me, "You know, that's been nagging at me for years." I answered that she was definitely not alone.*

If you have a minor child, or children, you automatically have estate planning concerns. Who will raise your child if you can't? More precisely, if you and the child's other parent, if there is one involved, die before your child is a legal adult (over 18), who will be the adult responsible for caring for the child? Legally, there are two different adult roles involved. The first is raising and nurturing the child—having legal custody, and making day-to-day personal decisions on the child's behalf. The second adult role is managing any property owned by, or left for the use of, the child. Minors cannot, by law, control any significant amount of property they own. Commonly, parents name one adult to serve in both capacities.

Example: *Felicity and Joe have two young children, ages one and three. They own an inexpensive car, personal and household belongings and two life insurance policies for $100,000, one on each spouse's life. If one parent dies, the other one will, of course, carry on. But like many parents, the couple worries about what will happen if they die together. They discuss who should raise their children and manage the insurance money if they both die. They are pleased and relieved to agree that their wisest choice is Joe's sister Susan, who loves their kids and is securely married with one child of her own. Felicity and Joe discuss the matter with Susan, who agrees to serve as guardian if the need arises.*

Joe and Felicity also are aware that present stability is no guarantee of lifetime security. If Susan's life drastically changes for the worse, Joe and Felicity will then make new plans for the care of their children.

I'M NOT READY

I've thought of putting that phrase on my tombstone, though I decided instead to use what I cried out as a child whenever my parents asked me to do a chore: "Right Now?" But, all kidding aside, "I'm not ready" is how many people feel about estate planning. There are some understandable reasons for this procrastination: a busy life, a rational mistrust of lawyers, a sense that estate planning is boring. I suspect though that there's often something more primitive at work: at least a touch of superstition, a fear that thinking about death might somehow hasten its occurrence.

If you procrastinate until death, that will prove costly to your inheritors, and may well mean that your property will not be distributed as you wish. If you die without a will or other valid transfer device, your property will be divided between family members according to a formula established by state law. A judge will appoint someone of her choosing to supervise the distribution of your property. Your estate must pay this person's fee, which can become quite hefty.

Similarly, if you have minor children and the other parent is not available or suitable for custody, you won't want to take the chance that you'll have no input regarding who will raise the child if you can't.

In sum, ready or not, it's wise to get your estate planning done soon.

Basic estate planning has just a few branches. I'll sketch them out here; these subjects are then covered in more depth in subsequent chapters.

A. Choosing Your Beneficiaries

Your beneficiaries (W.C. Fields called them "bean-fisheries") are the people and organizations to which you leave your property. Distribution plans can range from the simple, such as leaving everything to your spouse, to far more complex arrangements, such as using trusts to leave property to many family members over generations, as well as leaving property to friends and organizations.

As I've said, you decide who gets your property. I've found that most people who start estate planning know who their beneficiaries will be. You're unlikely to need a lawyer's help here, as the most a good one could do is to help you clarify your own desires if you feel confused or conflicted, or perhaps point out some difficulties that might arise if you're considering a complex beneficiary plan. But most people face no serious problem here. The key components of a simple beneficiary situation are that your choices are clear, and that you leave your property outright, with no strings or controls attached. (One exception might be property left to minors or young adults. See Chapter 3, Section C.)

Example 1: *Francine and Phillip, a married couple, want to leave everything to each other. When the second spouse dies, all the property will be divided equally among their three children.*

Example 2: *Lily has a son, age nine, and a modest estate. She wants to leave most of her property to her son (in a trust), and the remainder to her friends Kelly and Gretchen.*

Example 3: *Angela has a substantial estate, and two children, ages 45 and 36. She wants to leave the bulk of her property equally to them, plus gifts of specific heirlooms to her sister and niece, and some cash to The Nature Society.*

Couples in second, or subsequent, marriages may face more difficult beneficiary decisions. If one or both spouses have children from a prior marriage, conflicting desires can arise. Spouses may feel torn between leaving property to children from a prior marriage and aiding the current spouse, along with any children from the new marriage.

Example: *Russell and Katy remarry in their 50s. Russell has two children, ages 25 and 28. Katy has a daughter who just turned 30. Russell's net worth is about $170,000; Katy's is about $260,000. They purchase a house together. Each contributes $60,000 for the down payment. Katy will pay roughly two-thirds of the mortgage payments and house expenses, because she earns considerably more than Russell.*

Both spouses feel strongly that when one spouse dies, the other should be able to continue to live in the house. But they also want their individual shares of the house to go to their own children after they both die. Neither wants to create the possibility that the child or children of the spouse who lives the longest could somehow end up owning the entire house. The couple must agree on how the house will be divided when both die, including how Katy's extra contribution for payments and expenses will be apportioned. Also, they must devise a legal mechanism to accomplish their goals.

The usual legal device for handling this kind of second-marriage issue is a particular type of trust, called a "marital property control trust." (See Chapter 10, Section A.)

B. Providing for Young Children

Parents raising young children are usually quite clear that their major estate planning concern is providing for the minors if the parents suddenly die. (To remind you once more, a minor is any child under age 18.) "Providing" means deciding both who will raise the child and who will manage any money or property that the child legally owns. It may also include making plans to have sufficient property to leave the child, such as buying term life insurance. These concerns are discussed in depth in Chapter 3, but because they are so central to many people, I'll focus on a few important points here.

1. Custody of Your Children

If the other parent is involved and survives you, that parent will normally take custody of the children. In your will, you can nominate someone to serve as the child's "personal guardian" if there is no other parent involved, whether because the parent has died or abandoned the child. Your nomination is not binding on a court, however, because children are not property, and cannot be willed to someone. But if custody is not contested, which is true for the great majority of cases where a child's parent or parents die, the judge will routinely confirm the expressed desires of the deceased parent.

Example: *Myron and Kim are divorced, but manage to cooperate without viciousness in raising their young son Lawrence. Each understands that if one dies before Lawrence turns 18, the other parent will have custody. Myron dies and Kim now has sole custody. In her will, she nominates her sister Polly to serve as Lawrence's guardian if she dies.*

It's very difficult to prevent a parent who has been involved in raising a child from gaining legal custody if the custodial parent dies. But if the other parent has not been involved in raising the child, or you believe that parent is not fit to have custody, there are steps you can take to try to prevent that parent from gaining custody. (See Chapter 3, Section A.)

2. Your Children's Property

Legally, minors cannot own any significant amount of property outright, more than $2,500 to $5,000 depending on the state. So you need to nominate an adult to supervise and manage any property owned by your child, including property you leave the child, other inheritances, or her own earnings. There are several different legal devices you can use to leave property to your young children. These are discussed in Chapter 3, Section C.

C. Transferring Your Property After You Die

To arrange for the transfer of your property to your beneficiaries after you die, you must use one or some combination of various legal devices. The two most popular are wills and living trusts. Deciding which transfer devices are best for you is the main technical aspect of basic estate planning, where law and legal documents come into play.

At this point, some estate planning books start insisting that you hire lawyers, warning of the disasters that will befall anyone so daring as to try to handle his or her own affairs without paying thousands of dollars for professional help. As I've already stressed, this is nonsense. Most readers will learn that, applying their own common sense, they can safely select which device or combination of devices is best for them, without the cost of a lawyer.

1. Wills

A will, the simplest estate planning device to prepare, is a document that leaves some or all of your property to beneficiaries you choose. You can also use a will to name an adult guardian for your young children. Wills are discussed in detail in Chapter 4.

The principal drawback of a will is that it must normally go through probate, a complicated and expensive court proceeding. Probate rarely provides any real benefit to your beneficiaries, or, indeed, to anyone, except the lawyers involved. (See Chapter 4, Section D.)

2. Living Trusts

A living trust is a legal document similar to a will in function, except that no probate or other court proceedings are required to turn property over to beneficiaries. Because of this, living trusts are the most popular probate-avoidance device. (See Chapter 5.)

3. Other Ways to Transfer Property

There are a number of other ways to transfer property—and avoid probate—that can be useful in certain situations. These methods include:

- pay-on-death accounts for bank deposits or securities (stocks and bonds)
- joint tenancy, a form of ownership where the surviving owner(s) automatically receive the interest of a deceased owner without probate, and
- tenancy by the entirety, a special version of joint tenancy specifically limited to married people.

These and other easy ways to avoid probate are discussed at greater length in Chapter 6.

D. Estate Taxes

The federal government imposes an estate (death) tax on the property of all U.S. citizens, and all property located in the U.S. owned by non-citizens. But the good news is that federal law exempts a large amount of property from taxation. In 1999, your estate will be taxed only if it exceeds $650,000 (net). The amount of this exemption will rise over a period of years until it maxes out at $1 million for 2006 and thereafter. (See Chapter. 8, Section A.)

The majority of states impose no death tax. In states that do, you can't do much about them, unless you have the option to move your primary residence to another state.

Only a small percentage of estates, less than 2%, pay federal estate tax. If your estate won't have to pay federal tax, you obviously have no need for the kinds of complex, expensive estate tax planning often undertaken by wealthier people. But if you conclude that your estate is likely to be large enough to incur tax, you should definitely explore ways to avoid, or at least reduce, that tax. (See Chapter 9.)

Also, if you're married, you should consider estate tax reduction methods if the combined estate of you and your spouse is likely to be subject to tax. Why? Because often each spouse wants to leave all of his or her property to the other. If that occurs, the total amount of the property the surviving spouse owns may become subject to tax, even though each spouse's original estate was well below the tax threshold. If the surviving spouse's estate is likely to be taxed when both estates are combined, there's a well-established type of trust, called an AB trust, that can reduce or eliminate tax risks. (See Chapter 9, Section B.)

E. Planning for Incapacity

Some people worry that there's much more to basic estate planning than leaving property to beneficiaries and arranging for the care of young children. Actually, little more is needed. The most important remaining task is making arrangements for the handling of your medical and financial affairs if you ever become incapacitated and can't handle them yourself.

When thinking about medical care, know that you have the legal right to specify in writing what types of treatment you want and do not want if you are in a coma or have a terminal condition. This document, commonly known as a "living will," more often called a "Healthcare Directive" or "Directive to Physicians," is binding on doctors, hospitals and all medical personnel. You also have the legal right to appoint a person of your choice to make medical decisions on your behalf if you cannot make them yourself. To do this, you must create a simple legal document called a durable power of attorney for healthcare.

Similarly, you can give someone you trust the authority to handle your finances if you become incapacitated and cannot handle them yourself. You do this by creating a durable power of attorney for finances. All of these arrangements are discussed in more detail in Chapter 11.

Beyond this, there isn't much more you need to do to plan your estate. There are, as I've said, related but separate areas of concern, from providing for retirement to worries over nursing homes and federal eligibility rules for Medicare. But for basic estate planning, I conclude this chapter as I began: You can understand it, and get it done without spending hours and hours of your time, or hundreds and hundreds of your hard-earned dollars.

F. Making Changes

You are not locked into anything when you prepare your estate plan, including your basic documents, such as your will or living trust. With a couple of exceptions, you can change, amend or revoke your documents any time you want to, for any reason—or for no reason. (Joint tenancy is a special case; see Chapter 6, Section D. Also, some types of estate tax saving trusts must be irrevocable while you live. See Chapter 9, Section C.)

The only limitation is that you must be "competent" when you make a change. Legally, "competence" means having the mental capacity to make and understand decisions regarding your property. You have to be pretty far gone before you aren't legally competent to change your documents. For instance, forgetfulness, including not always remembering who people are, does not by itself establish mental incompetence.

SOME THOUGHTS ABOUT DEATH

While this book concentrates on practical matters, I want to acknowledge the deepest reality involved—death itself.

We all experience the loss of family and friends; it's the human condition. Some years after his death, I continue to feel recurrent grief and loss at the tragic, unfathomable (to me) death of my friend (and fellow Nolo author) Hayden Curry.

Coping with death of a loved one is intensely personal. Some people are fortunate to have religious beliefs, traditions, rituals and ceremonies to help. Others find sources of solace and inspiration in nature, or from sacred works, or poetry. This is not a book of philosophy or religion, so I merely note that each person must seek to find his or her own acceptance—if not understanding—of death.

However you are able to deal with the fact of death, it's no denigration of that reality to arrange for your desired handling of your affairs after your death. After all, the effects of sensible estate planning benefit the living. Estate planning is a type of gift to those you love.

The people I've been close to who have died all prepared thorough estate plans. I saw and understood how important it was for them to know that they hadn't left a mess for their friends and family to clean up, and that they had directed that their property go where they thought it would be most beneficial.

G. More Estate Planning Resources from Nolo

At Nolo we are, of course, in favor of do-it-yourself law and avoiding lawyers whenever that's feasible. Below is a list of Nolo products that are useful for different aspects of estate planning and related matters.

- *Plan Your Estate* offers in-depth coverage of all significant elements of estate planning, from simple wills to complex tax-saving trusts, from funerals to family businesses.

- *WillMaker* (software for Windows or Macintosh) enables you to prepare a comprehensive will using your computer. It includes basic trusts for your minor children, allowing you to specify the age at which your children inherit property you leave them. *WillMaker* also allows you to prepare a healthcare directive, durable powers of attorney for healthcare and finances, and a document setting out your wishes for final arrangements.

- *Nolo's Will Book* provides in-depth explanation of how to prepare a will that covers all normal needs, including basic trusts for your minor children. Will forms are available as tear-outs or on a computer disk included with the book.

- *The Quick and Legal Will Book* enables you to prepare a basic will efficiently.

- *Living Trust Maker* (software for Windows or Macintosh) allows you to prepare a probate-avoidance living trust (but not an "AB" estate tax-saving trust).

- *Make Your Own Living Trust* provides a complete explanation of how to prepare a living trust. The book contains forms and information allowing you to create a living trust and, for married couples, a tax-saving "AB" trust.

- *8 Ways to Avoid Probate* offers a thorough discussion of all the major ways to transfer property at death outside of a will.

- *9 Ways to Avoid Estate Tax* provides a thorough discussion of the most important ways to avoid or reduce federal estate taxes.

- *The Financial Power of Attorney Workbook* shows you how to prepare your own durable power of attorney for finances, and contains all the forms you need.

- *How to Probate an Estate* (California Edition) shows Californians how to handle normal probate without an attorney.

- *The Deeds Book* (California Edition) explains how to use deeds to transfer California real estate for estate planning purposes.

- *Beat the Nursing Home Trap: A Consumer's Guide to Assisted Living and Long-Term Care* is a practical guide that provides all the information you need to help make the best arrangements for long-term care. It shows how to protect assets, arrange home healthcare, find nursing and non-nursing home residences, evaluate nursing home insurance and understand Medicare, Medicaid and other benefit programs.

- *Social Security, Medicare and Pensions* shows you the way through the current maze of rights and benefits for those 55 and over, including Medicare, Medicaid and Social Security retirement and disability benefits, and age discrimination protections.

You can order any of these books direct from Nolo. A complete catalog of Nolo books and software is at the back of this book. And if you are Internet savvy, be sure to visit Nolo's online legal encyclopedia at **www.nolo.com**. You'll find free self-help information on a wide range of legal topics, including lots of material to help you plan your estate. ■

Your Beneficiaries

Here we reach the core of estate planning: deciding who will receive your property after you die. This can be a satisfying part of the estate planning process because you can contemplate the benefits your property will bring to the people or organizations you choose. When it comes to naming beneficiaries, you are free to make whatever decisions you wish, except that if you are married, in most states you must leave at least half of your property to your spouse.

For estate planning purposes, beneficiaries can be divided into two groups, depending on the rights you give them. "Direct beneficiaries" receive your property outright. "Alternate beneficiaries" receive property only if the direct beneficiary for that gift is not alive when you die. Below we'll take a closer look at beneficiary types, as well as possible beneficiary complexities.

A. Direct Beneficiaries

A direct beneficiary is a person or institution you name in a will, trust, or pay-on-death account to receive a gift of specific property. For example, if you leave your car to your daughter, she is a direct beneficiary. You can have as many different direct beneficiaries, for different gifts, as you choose.

DEFINITION: GIFTS

You leave your beneficiaries some type of property. I call this leaving them a gift. Lawyers often use words like "bequest" or "legacy." (The latter defined by Ambrose Bierce as "a gift from one legging it out of this veil of tears.") Of course, the word gift can also be used to mean property freely given from one living person to another, or to an organization. (See Chapter 9, Section A, for more information about making gifts of your property during life.)

Direct beneficiaries come in two types:

- primary beneficiaries—people or institutions named to receive specifically identified property, and

- residuary beneficiaries—people or organizations named to receive any property not specifically left to primary beneficiaries.

Example: *In her will Kira leaves her car to her friend Alice, her jewelry to her friend Dori and $10,000 to the Nature Conservancy. All these are direct primary beneficiaries. She leaves all other property subject to her will to her brother Tom. He is her direct residuary beneficiary.*

A SPOUSE'S RIGHT TO INHERIT PROPERTY

In the great majority of states, called "common law" states, your spouse has a legal right to inherit part of your property, generally one-half. Common law states are all states except Arizona, California, Idaho, Nevada, New Mexico, Texas, Washington and Wisconsin, which are "community property" states. (Alaska, though it is not generally a community property state, allows a married couple to create a written agreement or trust defining some or all of their property as community property.) In community property states, the basic rule is that each spouse owns one-half of all property acquired by either spouse during marriage. There are, of course, some exceptions. Major ones are property owned by one spouse before marriage and kept separate during the marriage, and property inherited by or given to one spouse.

In common law states, the owner of property is the person whose name is on the ownership document, such as the deed to a house. However, these states' laws protect a surviving spouse from being completely disinherited by the other spouse, no matter what the ownership documents state. If a spouse isn't left at least the amount required by state statute, usually one-half of the other spouse's property, the excluded spouse can claim that amount no matter what the other spouse's will provided. But in most all common law states, a spouse can waive his or her statutory inheritance rights. This can be done in a prenuptial agreement, or at any later time.

Leaving a Spouse Less Than Half of Your Property. *If you live in a common law state, and you want to leave your spouse less than one-half of your property, see a lawyer.*

Special Rule for Floridians. *The Florida Constitution (Art. 10, § 4) prohibits the head of a family from leaving a family residence in his or her will to someone other than a spouse or child, if either exist.*

As mentioned in Chapter 1, many people's beneficiary situations are simple. Even if you want to name many different beneficiaries for different specific items of property, your beneficiary plan can still be simple. As long as you clearly set out which person gets which item, there should be no trouble. Other people, however, don't have it so easy. One or more complicated questions may arise about possible beneficiaries. But before discussing these complexities, let's look at one concern you should consider no matter what your beneficiary situation: whether to name alternate beneficiaries.

B. Alternate Beneficiaries

An alternate beneficiary is a person or organization you name to receive a gift you left to a direct beneficiary, if that direct beneficiary dies before you, or does not outlive you by a defined period of time, often 30 to 45 days. (The latter is called a "survivorship requirement.") You can name one or more alternate beneficiaries for every one of your direct beneficiaries. Commonly, spouses who leave all of their property to each other name their children as alternate beneficiaries. Other alternate beneficiary plans can be more complex.

Example: *Howard leaves his property equally to his brother Al and sister Sheila. If Al dies before him, Howard decides to leave Al's property as follows: 25% each to Al's three children, and 25% to named charities. If Sheila dies before Howard, he names alternate beneficiaries and divides her share this way: 50% to her daughter, 25% to named charities and the remaining 25% to a political cause.*

When preparing your will or living trust, must you name alternate beneficiaries? The conventional estate planning advice is that you must. I disagree. Generally, naming alternate beneficiaries is wise. But it's not mandatory to name them in all situations.

If there's a reasonable chance that a primary beneficiary will not outlive you, for instance if the beneficiary is elderly or ill, it's surely sensible to name an alternate. Of course, you could amend your will or trust to name a new beneficiary for property left to someone who predeceases you, but naming alternates will save you the work. Also, it eliminates the risk that you won't be able to amend your will or living trust—or that you simply won't get around to it. Better to have a plan already in place, which means naming alternate beneficiaries.

So why would someone decide not to name alternate beneficiaries? Because naming alternate beneficiaries means considering horribles—someone you love dying before you do.

Example: *Demitrous, a widower, leaves all of his property to his daughter Irene. He refuses to contemplate her dying before him, and does not name an alternate beneficiary. The risk is that if she does predecease him, and he doesn't name a new beneficiary, his property will be distributed to his closest relations according to state law, which might not be what he wished.*

This example above is an extreme case, because there is only one beneficiary and no back up. Most people don't put all their eggs in one basket, so a more serious question is how far down the route of alternate beneficiaries they want to go. For instance, do you want to make a plan for what happens to a gift if both the direct and alternate beneficiaries die before you? What if all your children and grandchildren die before you?

I have six brothers and sisters, all healthy. My parents prepared a shared living trust in their early 70s. Each decided that they wanted to leave all their property to the other spouse. And each named all seven children as equal alternate beneficiaries. When one spouse died, the children would become the direct beneficiaries of the surviving spouse.

My parents did not want to name alternates to their children. I understood their decision. Neither wanted to imagine one of their children dying before both of them, and I certainly wasn't going to try to talk them into such morbid speculation.

Of course, some people want to carry out several levels of beneficiary planning, naming alternates for each alternate and so on. That's fine too. A primary purpose of estate planning is to give you peace of mind that as far as worldly property goes, you've prepared for the consequences of your death. If you are comforted by knowing that your planning will include what happens to your property if there are multiple tragedies, do that planning. The bottom line is that, as with all your basic estate planning decisions, you are your own expert, and can decide what feels right to you.

YOUR PROPERTY

You need to know what property you own in order to leave it. Most people, especially those doing basic estate planning, face no problem here. Their holdings are no mystery to them. Often a home is the major asset, then there's a car, some savings, perhaps stocks or other investments, and household possessions, including jewelry. And there may be other assets, such as funds remaining in retirement accounts like an IRA or a 401(k) plan, where beneficiaries are named as part of the asset. (Using retirement plans as estate planning devices is discussed in Chapter 7.)

You don't necessarily have to prepare an itemized list of your property to do your estate planning. Indeed, most people don't need to bother with it. However, you might find it helpful to inventory your property. This can be particularly desirable if:

- You plan to leave many items of property to many different beneficiaries—for example, a large collection of jazz records to be distributed between dozens of fellow aficionados.
- You are not sure what you actually own, perhaps because of shared business ownership, or because you're not certain about your state's rules governing marital property for estate planning purposes. For instance, in community property states, a few types of property acquired during marriage can be separate property, including inherited property left solely to one spouse, and earnings from separate property that are kept distinct from all shared property.
- You want to pin down what you own so you can estimate your net worth to see if your estate is likely to owe federal estate tax. But even here, a rough estimate of total value is all you need, and you may not have to itemize meticulously to make that estimate.

If you decide you do need an itemized list of your property, Nolo's hands-on estate planning resources provide thorough checklists of all significant types of property so you won't overlook, say, your gas and oil royalties.

C. Beneficiary Complexities

Viewed pragmatically, estate planning is a mix of property, deep human emotions and law. The legal devices should not be intimidating. As I've urged, you can master them well enough to do your own basic planning. It's the blend of property and emotions that can cause serious problems. Money may not be *the* root of all evil, but it's high on the list. Of course, few people worry about evil when doing their planning. But many are concerned with how to distribute their property fairly, or how to prevent, as best they can, future conflicts over that property.

Ultimately, these are personal matters, not to be left to estate planners—certainly not me. However, I can offer some examples of beneficiary complexities and solutions drawn from the real life (sometimes, too-real life) of my estate planning practice.

1. Simultaneous Death

Many couples, especially those with small children, are concerned about what will happen if both die at the same time. Sure, they know that this is highly unlikely, but that doesn't negate the genuine worry.

With young children, the person named by both parents as the children's personal guardian steps in to raise the children. (Each member of a couple should choose the same adult as personal guardian; this is discussed in Chapter 3, Section A.)

A potential problem can arise with property. Suppose one spouse lived five minutes longer than the other? Or suppose it can't be determined which spouse outlived the other? What is the best way to ensure that property is left the way each spouse intended?

There are two methods used to make sure each spouse's property wishes are followed:

- A "survivorship clause" is imposed over all gifts, including those to a spouse, requiring each beneficiary to outlive the giver by a set period, often 30 or 45 days. If the beneficiary does not survive this period, the gift goes to the alternate beneficiary.
- Each spouse's will and living trust contains a "simultaneous death clause," which provides that when it's difficult or impossible to tell which spouse died first, the property of each spouse is disposed of as if he or she had survived the other.

Logically inclined readers may wonder how this can work. How can I be presumed to have survived my wife when she's presumed to have survived me? Yes, it's a paradox, but it's allowed because it works to get the desired results. Technically, the argument is that each spouse's property is handled independently of the other. In reality, as the oft-cited quote of Oliver Wendell Holmes explains, "The life of the law has not been logic, it has been experience."

Example: *Guillermo and Venus are killed in a plane crash. Each had a will leaving all property to the other. Guillermo's alternate beneficiaries are his brother and sister. Venus' alternate beneficiary is her daughter from her first marriage. Each will contains a simultaneous death clause. For property distribution purposes, Guillermo's will is treated as if he survived Venus, so his property goes to his brother and sister. Similarly, Venus' will is treated as if she survived Guillermo, so her property goes to her daughter.*

2. Second or Subsequent Marriages

"Blended" families, or sometimes not-so blended families, can raise complex and difficult estate planning concerns. People who've married more than once may have trouble reconciling their beneficiary desires for their present spouse (and family, if the couple has children from their present relationship) with their wishes for children from their prior marriages. Individual situations can vary greatly, often depending on whether marriages occurred relatively early or late in life and on how well family members get along. But one thing is obvious—if yours is a non-traditional family, you must carefully consider, and do your best to reconcile, needs that may be competing and conflicting.

Often the main problem is how to provide for your current spouse while still keeping the bulk of your property intact for your children. A trust can be very useful here. (See Chapter 10, Section A.)

3. Unmarried Couples

Unmarried couples have no legal right to inherit each other's property. A central concern of most members of unmarried couples is to arrange to leave property to the other. Happily, unmarried people—whether lesbian, gay or heterosexual—have the right to leave their property to whomever they want, using a will or other transfer device like a living trust. In case of serious threat by hostile family members, a member of a couple may take action to establish by clear proof that she or he was mentally competent when the estate plan was prepared.

Example: *Ernest and Linda have lived together for many years. Aside from a few small gifts to friends or family, each wants to leave all property to the other after death. They're concerned with efficiency and economy, but above all they want to be sure that their estate plan can't be successfully attacked by several close relatives who have long been hostile to their lifestyle. Ernest and Linda each prepare a living trust leaving their property as they desire. They videotape their signing and the notarization of this document, and have two witnesses watch them sign, to provide additional proof that they were both mentally competent and not under duress or undue influence when they finalized their documents.*

4. Unequal Distribution of Property

Parents, or a parent, may want to leave property unequally between two or more children. This is perfectly legal. The problem is what the kids may think and feel about it.

Example 1: *Gunnar and Louise are married, with a modest estate. They have two children in their twenties, Andrea, in her first year of medical school, and Suzanne, who's happily married to a rich man. Each spouse leaves all his or her property to the other. The alternate beneficiaries, who will receive the property when both spouses die, are their children.*

Gunnar and Louise decide that they will leave 75% of their property to Andrea, who faces many more years of financial strain before she becomes a surgeon. But the couple is also aware that they may need to revise their plan after Andrea achieves her goal, or if Suzanne encounters financial stresses. Also, they decide they want to explain their decisions to both daughters, to see if all agree that the plan is fair.

Example 2: *Sherry has three children: Patricia, a prosperous lawyer, Albert, a successful journalist, and Caroline, a dancer and single mother. Sherry decides she will leave most of her estate to Caroline, because she's the only child who really needs financial help. Sherry decides to talk to all three children together, to discuss what percentage to leave to each child, and the circumstances under which she'd change her property distribution.*

These are nice tidy examples, but reality may be more murky. Perhaps children who receive less than an equal portion will feel disturbed or resentful for any of a number of reasons. Perhaps not every conflict can be resolved by one amicable discussion. Sometimes, a major part of estate planning is facing that there are serious conflicts between your beneficiaries, or even in you, about the distribution of your property.

5. Shared Gifts

You can name more than one beneficiary for a gift. Indeed, you can name as many beneficiaries as you want to share a gift.

When naming shared beneficiaries, you need to resolve two key questions. First, what does each beneficiary receive? This is normally handled by leaving percentages of the gift to each recipient.

Example: *"I leave my house to my children as follows:*
35% to Alexis
25% to Constance
25% to Edward
15% to Phyllis."

Next, you need to decide if the gift should be sold promptly after you die, and the proceeds divided between the beneficiaries in the percentages you specified, or if your beneficiaries are to share ongoing ownership of the property. This latter alternative raises some thorny problems—for example, how will the beneficiaries share control or management of the asset and what will happen if one or more beneficiaries wants to sell? You must consider possible conflicts between your beneficiaries—not abstract possibilities of conflict, which always exist short of paradise, but difficulties that might actually occur. In Yeat's phrase, "cast a cold eye" on the characters, and relationships, of your beneficiaries. A gift with continuing shared ownership is a good idea only if you are confident that there won't be significant conflict between them.

Example: *Lewis wants to leave the family house equally to his three adult children. He doesn't want them to sell the house because one child, Joe, who's had money and work problems, lives there for free. But Lewis also knows that another child feels Joe is a moocher and needs to grow up. Also, Lewis doesn't want to let Joe live in the house forever for free, depriving the other two children of their inheritance. Lewis needs to resolve whether he really wants to* *leave the house with continuing shared ownership, or simply order it sold, and possibly leave more than one-third of the proceeds to Joe.*

Getting Help With a Shared Ownership Plan. *If you want to leave a gift that involves ongoing shared ownership, consider seeing a lawyer to work out the terms and form of that ownership. You might want to provide some rules to govern ownership, including possible disputes. And leaving the property in a trust can be an effective way to create binding rules, but this kind of trust requires careful individual attention.*

6. Long-Term Care for a Child With Special Needs

Parents of mentally or physically disabled children may need to provide care and support for those children whether they are minors or adults. Providing this care often requires the help of experts, particularly to coordinate the parents' support with rules on government benefits. Usually, parents must create a long-term trust to achieve their goals. (See Chapter 10, Section B.) Also, it may be that, in their estate planning, parents, must concentrate most of their resources on their disabled child, leaving less for any other children.

Example: *The Balfour family has a disabled child, Bob, age 15, who will need care all his life. They have two other children, both of whom are healthy. The Balfours' primary estate planning concern is doing all they can to arrange for Bob's care after they die. They realize this means leaving Bob most of their modest estate. They discuss this with their 19-year-old daughter, Rebecca, who says that's fine. Their other son, Jeb, resents the attention Bob gets and isn't so acquiescent. But the Balfours decide that protecting Bob remains their top priority. They hope that, as Jeb matures, he will understand the difficulties Bob faces and that his resentment that Bob got more than his share of parental attention (as Jeb defines it) will fade.*

There are many questions the parents must resolve about Bob. Who will be responsible for his personal care after they die? How can they best leave money for Bob's use? How will any money they leave be treated when determining eligibility for government benefits? After all, it makes no sense to leave money to Bob if it means he will be ineligible for government help until it's all used up. The Balfours must chose a personal guardian to be responsible for Bob until he becomes a legal adult, at age 18, and a financial guardian or manager to supervise any money they leave for Bob, as long as Bob lives.

The Balfours discuss these concerns themselves and then broaden their discussion to include Rebecca, other family members and close friends they are considering for these two tasks. Eventually, they choose Mrs. Balfour's younger sister to be Bob's personal guardian if needed. They name their closest friend, William, to be Bob's financial manager, until Rebecca turns 30. After that, she will become Bob's financial manager.

To understand how to dovetail money they leave Bob in trust with government benefits, the Balfours do some preliminary research. They decide to establish a "special needs" trust for Bob. An expert lawyer drafts this trust, designing it to maintain Bob's eligibility for government assistance programs and to provide control for the trustee (the property manager) over trust property used for Bob's benefit.

7. Placing Controls on Gifts

For one or more reasons, you may want to impose controls on your gifts, rather than leaving them outright to beneficiaries. Leaving shared ownership is one form of control. Others include leaving property to someone who is unable to manage it, or trying to control what happens to property for a long time after your death. The usual way to impose control over a gift is through a trust. (See Chapter 10.)

You do need to find out whether the controls you want are legal—and feasible. First, you should know that you can't legally control your property for many generations. The basic legal rule is that you can impose controls for a maximum period of "lives in being" (that is, people alive now) plus 21 years. Further, some controls are too difficult to enforce. For example, suppose you leave a gift to someone only if he quits smoking. Who is to police that person? For how long must he quit smoking? What happens if he doesn't? Trying to impose moral requirements on your beneficiaries simply won't work.

This just scratches the surface how difficult it is to try to control someone's behavior in any way after your death. (Indeed, it's hard enough to have any control while you're alive.) Except for trusts for minors (see Chapter 3) and a couple of standard property control trusts (discussed in Chapter 10), it's wiser to accept that you can't shape other's actions once you're in the grave than to spend a lot of money for a lawyer-drafted trust that merely offers the illusion that you can.

D. Disiniheritance

You have no legal duty to leave anyone property, except your spouse in common law states. (See Section A, above.) Indeed, except for your children, you don't have to expressly disinherit others; anyone not mentioned in your will has no right to any of your property. You do have the legal right to disinherit any child—regardless of whether others think it's sad—but you must clearly express that intention in your will.

Most states have laws to protect children of any age from being accidentally disinherited. If a child is neither named in your will nor specifically disinherited, these laws provide that the child has a right to a portion of your estate. In many states, these laws apply only to children born after you made your will, but in a few states they apply to any child. And in some states, these laws apply not only to children but to any grandchildren of a child who has died. For this reason, if you want to disinherit a child, it's critical that you state this directly in your will.

LAWSUITS AGAINST YOUR ESTATE

Some people worry that their will or living trust will be legally challenged by a disgruntled would-be inheritor, or a beneficiary who didn't get what he or she expected. First of all, it's important to realize that this rarely happens. Almost all wills and trusts are handled without lawsuits. Next, as mentioned, no one but your spouse (and a child not expressly disinherited) has a legal right to any of your property. Still, some people fear that there are so many technicalities to a will or living trust that's it's difficult to get it done right, at least without paying a small fortune to a lawyer. This simply isn't true. Wills and living trusts have a few formalities, but only a few. With proper instructions and well-drafted forms, it's not a big deal to get it done right.

Others worry that, even if technically sound, their will or living trust could be invalidated in court. This also is not true. A court will invalidate a will or living trust only if it finds that the person who made it was mentally incompetent, or that the document was "procured" (obtained) by fraud or duress. Fraud means things like giving someone a paper to sign that the signer thinks is, say, a letter, but later turns out to be a will. Duress means undue pressure or coercion.

Fraud or duress are hard to prove, even when they actually happen. And they are almost impossible to prove if they didn't happen. Of course, under our legal system, it's not hard to file a lawsuit challenging a will or trust. These days, you can find a lawyer to file just about anything. But a frivolous lawsuit is not cause for big worry, though it may indeed be some hassle to your inheritors.

If You Fear a Lawsuit. *If you think anyone might file a lawsuit against your will or living trust, see a lawyer. There are steps you can take to diminish the chances that a lawsuit would be successful.*

E. Talking it Over

You may want to talk about your estate plans with close family members or other key beneficiaries, in the hope of making property transfer smoother after you die. Talking things over can be as simple as telling your beneficiaries what you've done. Or you can expand your discussions, and take your beneficiaries into the planning process.

1. Consider Discussing Your Plan

In my view, if you think you can safely discuss what you've done with your closest family members or other prime beneficiaries, it's a very good idea to do so. After all, they'll find out eventually, so why keep it a secret now? I know families where serious emotional damage was done—or compounded—by keeping estate planning secrets. One friend, who'd been raised in near poverty and whose parents continued to live a life of penury, was shocked and hurt (as well as pleased) when he learned that his inheritance was over $400,000.

Even in less extreme situations, keeping your plans a secret may raise serious questions. Why the need for secrecy? If there's something to be faced, consider dealing with it while you live—and can have some input into things. On the other hand, communication is not always a cure-all. If, after reflection, you decide that you don't want to reveal your plan—well, it is your plan, and (to stress it yet again) there ain't any must-do rules here.

2. Talking As Part of the Planning Process

Some people decide to include close beneficiaries in their planning process. Among other benefits, this may help you clarify your decisions.

Example: *A couple of my siblings have done, as it's said, "very well." And my parents, though far from rich, wound up, through decades of prudence and hard work, with an estate far larger then they'd imagined. One prosperous brother generously suggested to my mother that they not leave him any money, because he had plenty. My mother asked what I thought. I answered what I was sure she thought: leave us all the same percentage. She instantly agreed. Symbolically, she did not want to differentiate in inheritance between any of her children. I concurred, adding that, after all, I had chosen to be a renegade legal writer rather than an affluent corporate lawyer. Why should I get more than my brother because I had made what was, for me, a good choice?*

From another perspective, part of the satisfaction of estate planning can be asking those you love what specific items of yours they want. Further, perhaps you'll be fortunate and there will be no conflicts over heirlooms—but if there are, you can resolve them now, while you're alive.

Example: *My frugal mother somehow managed to purchase a number of fine etchings during the 1940s and 1950s. Rather than simply leave them for the kids to divide up after her death, my mother asked us to go through them and select at least one that we wanted. This was not a tightly structured process. During a visit to our old home, one or another of us would look at the etchings and choose. There was some overlap of choices, but nothing we couldn't work out.*

Through her giving, my mother not only had the pleasure of anticipating who would have which etching, but she's also had the fun of going through them several times, and going through them with children who've loved at least some of them since childhood. ■

Children

In estate planning, the word "children" can have two meanings. The first is "minors"—individuals who are not yet 18. The second meaning is offspring of any age; parents who live long enough can have "children" who are in their 40s, 50s or even older. This chapter focuses primarily on minor children because that's such a vital concern for so many parents. I also briefly discuss ways to leave property to a young adult child, when you're concerned that the child may not be sufficiently mature to handle money responsibly. Finally, I cover leaving property to other people's children.

Most parents of minor children are understandably concerned with what would happen to their children if disaster strikes and the parents die. If both parents are raising the children, this concern usually centers on simultaneous death of the parents. If you're a single parent and the other parent is deceased, has abandoned the child or is unavailable for some other reason, the worry is what will happen to your child if you die before the child reaches adulthood.

REVISE YOUR ESTATE PLAN TO INCLUDE NEW CHILDREN

If, after preparing your estate plan, you have or adopt a new child, revise that plan by providing for her or him. Naturally, you'll want to do this. But if somehow you don't get around to it, that child has a legal right to inherit a portion of your property. (See Chapter 2, Section D.) The percentage of your estate that this child would take by law might not be what you desire. And a legally mandated inheritance could upset your estate plan in other ways. For example, you might want your new child, along with other children, to be an alternate beneficiary, with no inheritance rights if your primary beneficiaries survive you. Whatever your wishes, it's best to revise your plan and put them in writing.

A. Naming Someone to Care for Young Children

If two parents can care for a minor child, and one dies, normally the other has the legal right to assume sole custody. Even if the parents are divorced or never married, as long as both parents are participating in raising their children, this rule presents no problem. But what happens if both parents die? Or a sole parent dies? Or a custodial parent believes the other should never have custody of the children?

First, some legal rules. Every minor must be raised by an adult who is legally responsible for the child's care. If there are no parents capable of handling this responsibility, another adult, called the child's "personal guardian," will be appointed by a court. In your will, you can nominate someone to be your child's personal guardian, and a back up, called the successor personal guardian. If you have young children, this is a major reason why a will is essential.

The person you name as personal guardian cannot actually serve as the legal guardian until approved by a court. The judge has the authority to name someone else if the judge is convinced it is in the best interests of the child. This may seem outrageous to you—how could a judge have authority to go against your own choice of the best guardian for your child? The short, legal answer is that children are not property and cannot simply be "left" to someone as, say, a diamond or an automobile can. That said, the reality is that if, as is usually the case, no one contests your choice for your child's personal guardian, a court will almost certainly confirm this person. In practice, a court will reject an unopposed nominee only if there are grave and provable reasons to do so, such as a serious criminal background, child abuse or dangerous self-destructiveness, such as drug addiction.

1. Choosing Your Child's Personal Guardian

You may well know whom you want to name as your child's personal guardian. For many parents, there's one obvious choice—an adult who is willing to accept the responsibility, and would love and care for the child. Other parents have to struggle to decide on a personal guardian. Sometimes two parents don't initially agree on who is the best choice. And other times, both for couples and single parents, there appears to be no good choice. But however you get there, you do need to make a decision—and then resume living with the faith that the person you named will never need to serve. You should always name a successor personal guardian as well, in case your first choice is unable to serve or to continue to serve.

In many families today, children don't all share the same two biological parents, and you may not want to name the same guardian for each of your children. Naming different personal guardians for different children is certainly legal. A court would likely follow this arrangement, unless there's persuasive proof that it would be harmful to a child. It can be helpful to attach a statement to your will, setting out why you've chosen the guardians you have. A court isn't required to follow this statement, or even accept it as valid evidence, but a conscientious judge will surely consider it.

Example: *Janine has custody of her two daughters, aged 14 and 15, from her first marriage, and her son, age 6, from her second. Her first husband has never taken any interest in, and little responsibility for, the girls. Her second ex, Todd, has been an adequate, though from Janine's view, well below superb, father to their son, and has also tried to be decent to her daughters. While all three children would like to stay together, Janine reluctantly recognizes that this can't be paramount in her decision. Janine's sister, Brenda, is close to the daughters and would, Janine strongly believes, be a much better personal guardian for them than Todd. But Todd would certainly want and be entitled to custody of their son.*

Janine names Brenda as guardian for her daughters—and successor guardian for her son if neither she or Todd is alive. Finally, she names Todd as successor guardian for the girls. She then attaches a statement to her will explaining why she believes this arrangement is best for her children.

2. If You Don't Want the Other Parent to Become Personal Guardian

A parent raising a child may not want the other parent to have custody, for any of a number of reasons. The custodial parent may believe that the other parent is dangerously destructive, emotionally or physically. Or a custodial parent may have remarried, and may believe that his current spouse is a far better parent to his children than his ex.

Clearly, one parent should not lightly attempt to deprive the other of custody. But when strong reasons compel a parent to nominate someone else to be personal guardian, what will happen if the custodial parent dies and the custody issue is presented to a judge? There is no definitive answer. If the other parent doesn't contest the deceased parent's wishes, the court will almost surely follow those wishes. ("Almost surely" is as certain as you ever get when it comes to courts.) But if the parent contests custody, a judge's decision would turn on both the facts of each situation and the judge's own beliefs. One general rule is that a parent cannot succeed in appointing someone other then the natural parent to be personal guardian, unless that parent:

- has legally abandoned the child, or
- is unfit as a parent.

It's usually quite difficult to prove that a parent is unfit, absent severe problems such as serious drug abuse, a history of violence to the child or mental illness.

It's unlikely that anyone except the child's other parent would win custody against your wishes. For instance, if you name your best friend Betty to raise your children if you can't, and Betty is clearly a caring adult, it's unlikely that someone else, such as the child's grandmother, or uncle, could gain custody over your choice.

Potential Custody Fights. *If you don't want the other parent to gain custody, discuss the details of your situation with a lawyer who specializes in family law.*

B. Naming Someone to Manage Your Child's Property

Minor children cannot own property outright, free of adult control, beyond a minimal amount—usually between $1,000 and $5,000, depending on the state. So, if you leave property to your minor child (whether as direct or alternate beneficiary), you must name an adult to be legally responsible for managing that property until the child becomes an adult. For now, let's call this adult your child's "property manager." You should also name a successor property manager, in case your first choice can't serve.

In contrast to a personal guardian, your appointment of a property manager and alternate is normally binding and not subject to court review. This is because a property manager controls only money and property, which you have a right to leave as you want.

LEAVING PROPERTY TO YOUR SPOUSE FOR THE BENEFIT OF YOUR CHILDREN

One option for parents of young children is for each to leave property outright to the other spouse to be used for their children's benefit. This approach makes sense if the parents trust each other, but obviously isn't desirable if the other parent is not available or is financially imprudent. Even if you leave all property to your spouse, it's always wise to name a backup property manager for your child. This ensures that the person you've chosen will manage your child's property if you and your spouse die simultaneously.

USING LIFE INSURANCE TO PROVIDE FOR YOUR CHILDREN

If you have young children but not much money, term life insurance can provide cash to support your children if you die while they are still young. Because term life insurance pays benefits only if you die during the covered period (often five or ten years), it's far cheaper than other types of life insurance. See Section D, below, for more information about naming your children as beneficiaries of life insurance.

The duty of your child's property manager is to manage property you leave for your children, or any other valuable property they acquire, honestly and in their best interests. This means using it to pay for normal living expenses and health and education needs. If you pick someone with integrity and common sense, your child's property should be in good hands. If substantial funds are involved, the property manager can pay for help to handle the more technical aspects of financial management. For instance, it's routine for a property manager to turn complicated tax and accounting matters over to an accountant.

When deciding on your minor child's property manager, here's a sensible rule: name the same person you choose as your child's personal guardian, unless there are compelling reasons to name someone else. For example, choose a different person if you're concerned that the personal guardian doesn't have sufficient financial or practical experience to manage property prudently. Similarly, for successor property manager, name the same person you designated as the child's alternate personal guardian unless there are strong reasons to choose someone else.

Obviously, the property manager must be willing to do the job, which might, depending on the ages of your children, last for many years. It's also wise to choose someone the other members of your family respect and accept. You want your children to inherit money, not family arguments.

Except as a last resort, don't name a bank or other financial institution to be property manager. Most banks won't manage accounts they consider too small to be worth the bother; as a rough rule, this means accounts worth less than $250,000. And even for larger estates, they charge hefty fees for every little act. In addition, it's my experience that banks are simply too impersonal to properly meet your own child's needs. Far better to name a human being you trust than a bureaucracy.

> **SELECTING DIFFERENT PROPERTY MANAGERS FOR DIFFERENT CHILDREN**
>
> In some situations, you may want to name different property managers for different minor children. Doing this is legal and does not require court approval.

C. Choosing How Your Children's Property Should Be Managed

You can choose the way property left to your children will be managed. You have three basic options:

- a custodianship, under what's called the "Uniform Transfers to Minors Act"
- a trust—either an individual child's trust for each child or a combined family pot trust, or
- a property guardianship.

1. The Uniform Transfers to Minors Act

A convenient device for leaving property to your child, by will or living trust, is the Uniform Transfers to Minors Act (UTMA), a law that has been adopted by every state except South Carolina and Vermont. Under the UTMA, your child's adult property manager is called a "custodian." You can choose any adult you want to be custodian. The custodian's management ends when the child reaches age 18 to 25, depending on state law.

Here's how leaving a gift using the UTMA works:

In either your will or living trust, you identify the property you want to leave to the minor, then name him or her as either direct or alternate beneficiary for that gift. Then you name the adult custodian, who is responsible for supervising the property until the child reaches the age at which he will receive the property outright. The custodian is entitled to reasonable compensation for her services; this payment comes out of the gift property. You also name a "successor custodian" in case your first choice can't do the job.

Example: *In her will, Pauline leaves $25,000 to her nephew Sacha. She completes an UTMA clause as follows: "All property I leave by my will to Sacha Pichiny shall be given to his father, Jules Pichiny, as custodian for Sacha Pichiny under the Uniform Transfers to Minors Act of New York."*

No court supervision of the custodian is required. The UTMA gives the custodian broad discretion to control and use the property in the child's interest. Because the UTMA is built into state law, financial institutions know about it, which should make it easy for the custodian to carry out property management responsibilities. The custodian must keep records so that tax returns can be filed on behalf of the minor, but no separate tax return must be filed for the UTMA assets.

As a general rule, the less valuable the property involved, the more appropriate the UTMA is. If the property will likely be used up by the time the child turns eighteen, or for college costs, using the UTMA is sensible. For example, given current college costs, you might leave a gift between $50,000 to $100,000 using the UTMA, in states where the beneficiary does not get property until he or she reaches 21.

2. Trusts for Children

A trust is a legal entity under which an adult, called a "trustee," has the responsibility of handling property in the trust for someone else, called the "trust beneficiary."

With a child's trust, your child is the beneficiary, and your child's property manager is the trustee. The trust document sets out the trustee's responsibilities and the beneficiary's rights, and the age at which the beneficiary is entitled to receive the trust principal outright.

STATES THAT HAVE ADOPTED THE UNIFORM TRANSFERS TO MINORS ACT

State	Gift Must Be Released When Minor Reaches Age:
Alabama	21
Alaska	18 (can be extended up to 25)
Arizona	21
Arkansas	21 (can be reduced to no lower than 18)
California	18 (can be extended up to 25)
Colorado	21
Connecticut	21
Delaware	21
District of Columbia	18
Florida	21
Georgia	21
Hawaii	21
Idaho	21
Illinois	21
Indiana	21
Iowa	21
Kansas	21
Kentucky	18
Maine	18 (can be extended up to 21)
Maryland	21
Massachusetts	21
Michigan	18 (can be extended up to 21)
Minnesota	21
Mississippi	21
Missouri	21
Montana	21
Nebraska	21
Nevada	18 (can be extended up to 25)
New Hampshire	21
New Jersey	21 (can be reduced to no lower than 18)
New Mexico	21

State	Gift Must Be Released When Minor Reaches Age:
New York	21
North Carolina	21 (can be reduced to no lower than 18)
North Dakota	21
Ohio	21
Oklahoma	18
Oregon	21
Pennsylvania	21
Rhode Island	18
South Dakota	18
Tennessee	21
Texas	21
Utah	21
Virginia	18 (can be extended to 21)
Washington	21
West Virginia	21
Wisconsin	21
Wyoming	21

STATES THAT HAVE NOT ADOPTED THE UTMA

At present, the UTMA has not been adopted in South Carolina or Vermont. Even if you live in one of these states, it is theoretically possible for you to use the UTMA in your will, if the minor or custodian or gift property itself resides in an UTMA state when you die. But for most parents, all these are and will likely remain in the state where they live. Even if one of them is now in an UTMA state, you don't know where it will be when you die. Committing yourself to this kind of updating is an unnecessary burden, since you can easily use a child's trust instead.

With a "family pot trust," the other major type of trust for children, two or more beneficiaries share rights to the principal of one trust. (There are other, more sophisticated trusts which can be used for children, such as a "special needs" trust for a disabled child, or a "spendthrift" trust for a child who simply can't handle money. See Chapter 10.)

Both a child's trust and a family pot trust are legal in all states. And like an UTMA custodianship, a child's trust or family pot trust can be established either by will or living trust. You select the adults you want to serve as trustee, and successor trustee. The trustee is entitled to compensation paid from the trust property, as provided in the trust document. Usually, the document simply states that the trustee may be paid "reasonable compensation" for services rendered. Trying to pin down a specific rate, or otherwise strictly control how much he is paid, indicates a mistrust of the trustee that should call into question whether a trust is desirable. If you don't completely trust your trustee, "dead-hand" control from a trust document is unlikely to solve real problems.

With either type of trust, the trustee manages the trust property, under the terms of the trust document, until it is turned over to the beneficiary or beneficiaries. Normally, the trustee may use trust assets for the education, medical needs and living expenses of a trust beneficiary.

a. The Child's Trust

With a child's trust, you leave specified property to one child. If you have more than one child, you create a separate trust for each one, with the result that each child's trust property is managed independently. You choose the age at which the child will receive the trust property outright. Often, a parent requires the child to reach age 25, or 35, or even older, before she or he is entitled to the property. So a child's trust is commonly used when a large amount of money is left for a child—more than the $50,000 to $100,000 that is appropriate for an UTMA gift.

Example: *Anita and Roberto have a ten-year-old daughter, LuAnne. Anita wants to leave her share of the house she co-owns with Roberto to LuAnne. But Anita does not want LuAnne to gain legal control over half-interest in the* *house until she is much older. So Anita leaves her share of the house in a child's trust, names Roberto as trustee, and specifies that LuAnne will not receive the trust property outright until she is 35.*

b. The Family Pot Trust

With a family pot trust, you leave property collectively for two or more children in one common fund; any amount of trust property can be spent for any child. In other words, the trustee doesn't have to spend the same amount on each beneficiary. Usually, the trust ends when the youngest child becomes 18. A pot trust is most often used by parents with younger children. These parents want to keep family money together, capable of being spent on any child as needs require.

Example *Sidney and Kim have three children, ages two, five and seven. Each spouse leaves all his or her property to the other spouse, with all three children as alternate beneficiaries. Property is left to the children in a family pot trust. Bob's brother Josh is named as trustee, and his wife Dianne as successor trustee. If both Sidney and Kim die while any of their children are minors, all family funds will be available for the children as needed—as they were when the parents lived.*

3. Naming a Property Guardian

In your will, you can name a "property guardian," who has authority to manage any of your minor children's property that doesn't come with a built-in adult manager. However, it is rarely, if ever, wise to leave property to your children that will be supervised by a property guardian. Here are several reasons:

- The property must go through your will, which means it is subject to probate. (See Chapter 4, Section E.)
- Property guardians are often subject to court review, reporting requirements and strict rules as to how they can expend funds.

All this usually requires hiring a lawyer and paying significant fees, but does little to guarantee that the property manager will do a good job. And those lawyer's fees, of course, come out of the property left to benefit the minor.

- A property guardianship must end when the minor becomes eighteen.

Still, you should name a property guardian (and successor) in your will to handle any property that belongs to your young children and isn't covered by some other legal device. Specifically, naming a property guardian in your will provides a supervision mechanism in case your minor children:

- earn substantial money after you die, or

- receive a large gift or inheritance that doesn't itself name a property manager.

Naming a property guardian also provides adult management in case you fail to include in an UTMA custodianship, child's trust or pot trust some property you leave to your kids.

D. Naming Children as Beneficiaries of Life Insurance

For many parents—most commonly younger parents who haven't acquired much property—life insurance is the major financial resource used to provide money for children in case one or both parents die. But if you name your children as beneficiaries, or alternate beneficiaries, of your policy, and you die while the children are minors, the insurance company cannot legally turn over the proceeds directly to them. If you haven't arranged for an adult to supervise the proceeds, court proceedings will be necessary to appoint and supervise a property guardian. As discussed above, this is not a good idea. Here are your options for avoiding that hassle:

- Name the children as policy beneficiaries and name a custodian under the UTMA for the proceeds. Most insurance companies permit this, and even have forms for it.

- Leave the proceeds to your children using children's trusts or a family pot trust as part of a living trust. (See Chapter 4, Section E.) You name your living trust (or the trustee, if that's what the insurance company prefers) as the policy beneficiary. You'll need to give a copy of your living trust to the insurance company, as well as complete any other paperwork they require. Then, in your living trust, you name the children as beneficiaries for any insurance proceeds that trust receives. You also create, as part of your living trust, children's trusts or a family pot trust to impose adult management over that gift.

It may not be possible for you to use your will to leave insurance proceeds in a child's trust or pot trust. Some insurance companies balk at this, on the grounds the trust won't come into existence until you die, and the policy beneficiary must be in existence when named. Rather than try to persuade an insurance company that this can be done, it's better to use a living trust to achieve your goal.

E. Leaving Property to Adult Children

If you believe one or more of your adult children is not capable of handling property responsibly, you can use one of several types of trusts to impose controls over his or her inheritance. Some of these trusts, such as spendthrift trusts or special needs trusts, are complex and must be drafted by a lawyer. (See Chapter 10, Sections B and D.) More commonly, you can use a child's trust to postpone the age at which your child receives property outright.

Example: *Franklin, a single parent, creates a living trust leaving his estate, worth $340,000, equally to his two children, Todd, 25, and Carolyn, 23. Todd has always been frugal with money, if not parsimonious. He's been saving since his first allowance. Carolyn is the flip side of the coin. She runs through whatever cash she has with speed and flamboyance, and from Franklin's perspective, often moves beyond generosity with money to recklessness. In his* *living trust, Franklin leaves Todd his half of the estate outright. However, he places Carolyn's half in a child's trust, with Franklin's brother Joe—a stable type if ever there was one—as trustee. Carolyn will not receive any trust property outright until she turns 35. By that age, Franklin hopes she will have become sensible enough to manage a large amount of money.*

This example is nice and simple (that's its point) but how desirable would it be in real life? Would Franklin—or you—really want to have one child's property held in trust while another child is left money outright? It's possible that such an arrangement would create emotional harm that far outweighs whatever fiscal prudence might be gained. So, once again, I stress that there are no rigid rules in estate planning. You always have to place legal options in the deeper context of human relationships.

F. Leaving Property to Other People's Children

If you want to leave property to minor or young adult children who aren't your own, whether your grandchildren or a child from another family, you have the following choices:

- You can leave small gifts—roughly worth under $2,000—directly to the child, if you believe he or she will handle the property responsibly.
- For larger gifts, you can leave the gift outright to the child's parent, and rely on the parent to use the gift for the benefit of the child.
- Leave the gift under the Uniform Transfers to Minors Act, discussed in Section C.1, above. This is best suited for gifts between $50,000 and $100,000. The child must receive the gift property outright at the age set by state law—21 in the majority of states, 18 in most others, and up to 25 in a few. You leave the gift to an adult custodian you name, who manages the property until it is turned over to the child.

- Create a child's trust for the gift. You name the trustee of each child's trust, to manage all property in it. Doing this makes sense for large gifts—those above the $50,000 to $100,000 you might leave under the UTMA. This method often makes good sense for large gifts to grandchildren, particularly if the trustee is the child's parent. (For more information, see Section C.2 if you're leaving property to a minor, or Section E if you want to leave property to a young adult.)

The least desirable method is simply to leave the gift in your will without selecting a method for adult supervision. In these circumstances, only five states allow the property to be turned over to the minor's parents, who hold the money for the benefit of the child until that child reaches age 18. These states are Delaware, Michigan (up to $5,000), New Jersey, New York (up to $10,000) and West Virginia. In states that have not adopted this sensible approach, court proceedings will be necessary to appoint a property guardian to supervise the gift. And because you are not the child's parent, you can't even appoint or suggest a property guardian for him or her in your will. ■

Wills

A will is what many people think of when they first consider estate planning. This makes sense. Everyone should have a will, whether or not they engage in more extensive estate planning. And many people decide that a will is all the planning they need, at least for the time being.

A will is simply a legal document, usually only a few pieces of paper, in which you name the people who will receive your property after you die (more accurately, all property left by the will). A will can also serve other vital purposes, such as appointing a personal guardian to raise your young children if you and the other parent aren't available. (See Chapter 3.) Wills do have a few technical requirements, but not as many as you might fear; you can readily master the technicalities.

You can name whomever you want as beneficiaries of your will property. And if your situation calls for it, you can establish a child's trust or a family pot trust in your will. (These trusts are discussed in Chapter 3.)

A. Will Requirements

Although most people know what a will is, at least in a general sort of way—something to do with property after a death—I've had a number of people tell me they don't really know what a will does, how it works, or what it requires. For example, they wonder if a will has to be typed or printed. And isn't there something about witnesses? Must a will be notarized? Filed with some judicial agency? Prepared with a valid stamp? Doesn't there have to be gobs of legalese in a will? Isn't it inherently dangerous to try to prepare a will without a lawyer?

Here's a short answer to each of these questions; I'll develop each answer later in this chapter. Yes, a will should be typed or printed. Yes, you must have at least two people witness your will. No, it does not have to be notarized. No, it does not have to be filed with some judicial agency—as long as you're alive. After you die, the will must go through a court proceeding called "probate." No stamp or other official imprimatur is required. And no, a will doesn't have to be gorged with legalese. Finally, for most people, there is no danger in preparing a will without a lawyer.

Though there aren't many formalities necessary to prepare a valid will, you do have to be sure your will complies with what is required. The problem here is that you can't rely solely on common sense. You must know the rules.

Example: *Ramona meant to prepare some kind of estate plan after her daughter, Laura, was born, six years ago. But neither she nor her partner, Ray, ever managed to get it done. Then Ramona got the chance to work at a film festival in Eastern Europe for three weeks. Only just before leaving did she type a letter, stating that if she died, she wanted her property used to take care of Laura. After she'd safely returned, she asked me if this paper would work as her will. After asking her some questions, I told her that, unfortunately, it wouldn't. She had failed to meet certain mandatory requirements for a document to be a valid will.*

Here are all the legal requirements for a valid will:

- You must be at least 18 years old.
- You must be "of sound mind." (The fact that you can read and understand this book is sufficient to establish that you are.)
- The document should be typed or computer printed. This is required in about half the states, and safest in all.
- The document must state that it is your will.
- You must leave some property to at least one beneficiary and/or appoint a personal guardian for any minor children.

- You must sign and date your will.
- There must be at least two witnesses (three in Vermont) who watch you sign your will and then sign it themselves. They do not have to know its contents.

Example: *To return to Ramona's letter, it fails to work as a will on several grounds. First, the letter didn't state that it was her will. Second, she had not dated the letter. Third, no one had witnessed the letter. Also Ramona had overlooked an important concern: Who should raise Laura if neither she nor Ray could?*

While there's no requirement that a will be notarized, you may decide to use a notary when your will is signed and witnessed. In almost every state, having the witnesses sign a brief statement called a "self-proving" affidavit, which is then notarized, can eliminate any need for a witness to testify at subsequent probate proceedings.

A WILL THAT LOOKS LIKE A "REAL WILL"

There are no appearance requirements for a will, beyond that it be legible. Physically, a will really is nothing more than some paper with typing or printing. But years ago, when I practiced law with two friends, we learned that some clients were disappointed at receiving a will that seemed so ordinary. So our flamboyant partner stapled each new will into a blue binder, closed this document with red ribbon and then sealed it with a red wax stamp. The wills looked vaguely aristo-cratic—or at least medieval—some clients were happier, and we charged more.

B. Your Executor

When you make a will, a primary task is appointing your "executor"—that is, the person with legal responsibility for carrying out the terms of the will. The executor (called a "personal representative" in some states) has legal authority to represent your estate, including supervising the distribution of property left by your will. Your executor may also have other tasks, ranging from locating will assets to filing estate tax returns.

AN EXECUTOR'S DUTIES

Executors can have a number of duties, depending on the complexity of the deceased parent's estate. Typically, an executor must:

- Decide whether or not probate proceedings are necessary. If the will property is worth less than a certain amount, formal probate may not be required. (See Section D, below.)
- If probate is required, file the will and all required legal papers in the local probate court.
- Manage the will property during the probate process, which may take up to a year.
- Set up an estate bank account, both for paying bills, and to hold money paid to the estate—for example, paychecks or stock dividends.
- Pay taxes, including a final income tax return for the deceased, and any federal or state estate tax return due.
- Supervise the distribution of the deceased's will property to the beneficiaries.

Your executor should be someone you trust and who's willing to do the job. You should also name a successor executor in case, for any reason, your first choice can't serve. If you plan to prepare a living trust, it's generally best that your executor be the same person you chose to be the successor trustee of your trust. (See Chapter 5, Section A.) Also, if possible, it's best to name an executor who lives in your state, or near it. A few states even require that the executor live in-state.

Out-of-State Executors. *In the following states, see a lawyer if you want to appoint an out-of-state executor: Florida, Illinois, Nevada, Ohio, Tennessee, Virginia, West Virginia.*

You can name co-executors, or even several executors, if you want to. Of course, it's simpler to name just one executor, but there can be compelling reasons—family harmony is one common example—for selecting more than one. If you have more than one, you must resolve whether any one of them can act independently on behalf of your estate, or if all (or a majority) must agree before acting. The first option has obvious risks, such as two trustees taking opposing actions, while the latter option can be very clumsy in practice, generating much paperwork. At the least, if you want multiple executors, be sure they all get along very well.

Some conventional estate planners recommend selecting a bank to be your executor. I strongly recommend against this, unless you have no other alternative. First of all, most banks won't take the job for a modest estate. More important, your executor is your link to the future, in charge of distributing your property after your death. You want someone human, with genuine concern, not an impersonal institution that charges fees for every small act. If your most trusted friend is your banker, name her as executor, but not the bank itself.

C. Types of Wills

Here I'll define the basic types of wills, other than the typed or computer printed varieties.

1. Handwritten Wills

A handwritten will (called "holographic" in legalese) must be written, dated and signed entirely in the handwriting of the person making the will. It does not have to be witnessed. Handwritten wills are recognized by about 25 states. But I definitely don't recommend them, even in the states where they're legal.

Handwritten wills aren't desirable because probate courts have traditionally been very strict when examining them after the death of the writer. Because a handwritten will isn't normally witnessed, judges sometimes fear that it might have been forged. Also, a judge may require proof that the will was actually and voluntarily written by the deceased person, which can be difficult to demonstrate. Hiring a handwriting expert isn't cheap. In short, given the tiny bit of extra trouble it takes to prepare a typed or printed will and have it witnessed, it's reckless not to do it.

2. Pour-Over Wills

A "pour-over" will directs that the property subject to it goes to (is "poured over" into) a trust. For example, sometimes people make their living trusts the beneficiaries of their wills. When the will property is poured over to the trust, the trust document controls who receives that property.

In my opinion, pour-over wills are usually not desirable. The purpose of a living trust is to avoid probate. (See Chapter 5.) Using a pour-over will simply ensures that some property that will eventually wind up in the trust must nevertheless go through probate. It's better to put property into the trust in the first place, when you create it.

However, a pour-over will can be helpful in a few situations. If you create a child's trust or a family pot trust in your living trust, you may want any will property to pour over to the living trust and become part of the property in the child's trust or family pot trust. (Child's trusts and family pot trusts are discussed in Chapter 3, Section C.) Otherwise, you'd have to set up two child's or family pot trusts—one in your will, another in your living trust. A pour-over will can eliminate this kind of wasteful duplication.

Example: *Ben and Mary create a shared living trust, each naming the other as primary beneficiary. Each also names their two young children as alternate beneficiaries. They create a family pot trust to hold any of the living trust property the children might inherit before the youngest turns 18.*

Ben and Mary each also create wills to transfer their cars, personal checking accounts, and a few other minor items. They make their wills "pour over" to their living trusts.

Ben and Mary die in a car crash, when their children are nine and 12. All property subject to their wills is poured into the living trust. Under the provisions of the trust, that property becomes part of the family pot trust to benefit the children.

Ben and Mary had to create only one family pot trust, because of their pour-over wills. Otherwise, each would have had to create three pot trusts, one in each will, another for the living trust property.

Candidly, it's my impression that some lawyers push pour-over wills because they not only sound sophisticated, they ensure that at least some probate fees can be collected.

3. Statutory Wills

A statutory will is a pre-printed, fill-in-the-blanks, check-the-boxes will form authorized by state law. California, Maine, Michigan and Wisconsin have statutory wills. In theory, statutory wills are an excellent idea—inexpensive, easy to complete and reliable. Unfortunately, in practice, statutory wills are so limited in scope that they aren't useful for most people. The choices provided in the statutory forms are quite narrow and cannot legally be changed—that is, you can't customize them to fit your situation or, indeed, change them at all. For example, the Michigan form allows you to make only two cash gifts (aside from household property); everything else must go to your spouse or children.

Normally, statutory wills are useful only if you are married and want all or the bulk of your property to go to your spouse—or, if she predeceases you, in trust for your minor children. Because of the limitations of statutory wills, the movement to introduce them in other states has stalled. No state had adopted a statutory will since the late 1980s.

4. Oral Wills

Oral wills (also called "nuncupative" wills) are not allowed in most states. In the few states where they are permitted, they are so restricted that they have little or no practical usage. For example, some states allow oral wills only if the willmaker spoke under the perception of his imminent death on a battlefield.

5. Video or Film Wills

Video or film wills are not valid under any state's law. It doesn't matter whether you think one would make sense. What works as a valid will is only what's authorized by state law.

Avoiding Lawsuits Over Your Will. *If you fear that someone may contest your will, ask a lawyer about using videotape or film to help establish that you were thinking clearly, and not under coercion, when your will was signed.*

D. Probate

Unless exempt under state law, all property left by will must go through probate, a tedious and expensive court process.

Many people, including, I'm sure, many readers of this book, wisely know they want the bulk, or even all, of their property to avoid probate. Indeed, far too many people have learned, often from bitter family experience, that the lawyer-infested probate process is costly, and time-consuming—and that it usually provides no benefits, except to attorneys.

Many people aren't sure what probate actually is, except that it involves lawyers, courts and transferring property after one's death. The actual probate functions are essentially clerical and administrative. In the vast majority of probate cases, there are no conflicts, no contesting parties—none of the normal reasons for court proceedings. Likewise, probate doesn't usually call for legal research, drafting or lawyers' adversarial skills. Instead, in the normal, uneventful probate proceeding, the executor provides a copy of the deceased person's will and other needed financial information to a lawyer, who then initiates the court proceeding. This drags on for months, or even years, as more papers are filed, notices sent out, routine hearings held, until a judge finally allows the will property to be distributed to the beneficiaries.

People who defend the probate system (mostly lawyers, which is surely no surprise) assert that probate prevents fraud in the transfer of a deceased person's property. In addition, they claim it protects inheritors by promptly resolving creditors' claims against the estate. In truth, however, very few estates or inheritors have any need for such "benefits," because it's the rare estate where there's any claim of fraud, or complicated debt problems. But if you have an estate with serious debt problems, including tax matters, you may want to leave your property by will, so that there's a forum for resolving these claims quickly.

PAYING BILLS

Even without major debt problems, almost everyone's estate will owe a few bills at least, ranging from credit card charges to routine household bills. If you want, in your will you can specify a source of funds to be used to pay any last bills. By contrast, many people simply decide to let their executor choose which estate money to use for paying final bills.

If you're leaving some of your property by will, it's sensible to do what you can to keep probate fees low. You cannot, unfortunately, make a legally binding contract with a lawyer to charge a low fee. Only your executor has legal authority to make a fee agreement with a probate lawyer, because the lawyer must be responsible to a living person.

SIMPLIFIED PROBATE FOR SMALL ESTATES

Some states don't require probate, or greatly simplify probate, for "small" or "modest" estates. Under some states' probate exemptions laws, a "modest" estate can have a substantial amount of money. In Oregon, an estate worth up to $140,000 is exempt from normal probate; in California, it's $100,000. If your estate qualifies for simplified treatment, there's no need to use any probate-avoidance device—a will is all you need.

In some states, probate fees are based on the value of the property subject to probate. Here you can obviously reduce the fees by reducing the probate estate's worth. In most states, however, probate fees are charged on the basis of the number of hours the probate lawyer works. Even here, if the estate is smaller, with few big-ticket items, less work should be needed and the fees should therefore be lower.

Ways to avoid probate are discussed in detail in Chapters 5 and 6.

PROPERTY TRANSFERS IN OTHER WESTERN COUNTRIES

Most western countries use the "civil law" system, which has a different base than our legal system. In these countries, including France, Spain, The Netherlands and Norway, there is no probate. Property transfers after death are very simple. No lawyer or judge is involved unless there is a conflict. Even England, from which we took our own messy probate system, abolished most court probate in the 1920s. Now, England is like the continental countries and transfers by a will are handled without lawyers and courts in almost all cases.

E. Using a Will in Your Estate Planning

Every estate plan should include a will. But how important that will is to the overall plan varies widely. Some people make a will their entire plan. For others, a will is only a small, but essential, part of it.

1. A Will as the Centerpiece of Your Estate Plan

Many people reasonably decide to make a will the centerpiece—or even, in some cases, the only piece—of their estate plan. They decide that, for the foreseeable future, a will accomplishes their estate planning goals. They can sensibly postpone more complicated, and perhaps more costly, estate planning work. You may be this kind of person if:

- No matter what your age or health, you simply don't want the bother of more extensive estate planning.

- You are healthy and statistically unlikely to die for decades. If you just want to be certain your basic wishes for your property are carried out in the very unlikely event you die suddenly, a will achieves this goal with less paperwork than other methods.

- Your primary estate planning goal is to ensure that if you die, your minor children are well cared for.

2. A Back-Up Will With a Comprehensive Estate Plan

There are lots of reasons to prepare a thorough estate plan: to avoid probate of most or all of your property, to reduce or eliminate estate tax or to address any of a number of other concerns. With a thorough estate plan do you still need a will? Definitely yes. Let's take an extreme case. Suppose you transfer every bit of your property by a living trust. Do you still need a will? Absolutely. It's always important to have at least a basic will, which I call a "back-up" will, as part of your estate plan for one or more of the following reasons:

To dispose of suddenly acquired property. Anyone may acquire valuable property at or shortly before death, such as a gift or inheritance, or even a lottery prize. Of course, it's sensible to promptly revise your estate plan to name a specific beneficiary to inherit this property. But what if you don't get around to it before you die? If you have a will, that property will go to your residuary beneficiary, who, by definition, takes "the rest of your (will) property"—that is, everything that isn't left to some other beneficiary.

To dispose of property not transferred by a probate-avoidance device. If you buy property but don't get around to planning probate avoidance for it—for example, by placing it in your living trust— a will is a valuable back-up device, ensuring that the property will go to your residuary beneficiary and not pass under state law. Similarly, if somehow you've failed to transfer some of your existing property to a probate-avoidance device—for example, because you didn't properly complete transfers of title—a will directs that property to your residuary beneficiary.

To name a personal guardian for your minor children. As I've already stressed, if you have minor children, you need a will to achieve the vital goal of naming a personal guardian for them. (See Chapter 3, Section A.) You can't use any other device for this purpose, except a living trust in a couple of states. Also, you can use your will to appoint a property guardian for your children, someone who will manage any of their property not otherwise legally supervised by an adult. (See Chapter 3, Sections A and C.)

In case probate is not required. As mentioned in Section D, above, small or modest estates may be altogether exempt from probate. In some states, even larger estates can benefit from probate-exemption laws. For example, in California, property transferred by probate-avoidance methods doesn't count toward the $100,000 limit. So even wealthy Californians can use a will for leaving lesser gifts—that treasured antique clock to a niece, $15,000 to friend, stock worth $18,000 to a fondly remembered employee—without ensnaring that property in probate as long as the total value left by will is under $100,000. The bulk of the estate, all property worth over $100,000, is transferred by probate avoidance methods.

To leave property you've inherited that is still in probate. On the off chance that someone leaves you property by will, and that property is still enmeshed in probate when you die, you need a will to specify who gets that property. Other transfer devices won't work.

3. Property You Can't Transfer by Will

Now that we've seen why a will is always a good idea, let's look at what types of property *cannot* be transferred by a will. A will has no effect on any property transferred by a valid probate-avoidance device. In other words, once you place property in one of the following forms of ownership, you cannot also leave that property by your will (not that you'd want to).

- **Property in a living trust.** It goes to the beneficiaries named in the trust document. (See Chapter 5.)

- **Property in a pay-on-death account, such as a bank account or stocks.** The person you designate as beneficiary on the account document inherits that property. (See Chapter 6, Sections B and C.)

- **Joint tenancy property.** At your death, your share automatically goes to the surviving joint tenants (but if all joint tenants die simultaneously, you can leave your share by will). (See Chapter 6, Sections D and E.)

- **Life insurance proceeds payable to a named beneficiary or beneficiaries.** The proceeds go directly to the beneficiaries. (See Chapter 6, Section H.)

- **Assets remaining in individual retirement programs, including IRAs, 401(k)s and profit-sharing plans.** The balance is payable directly to your named beneficiaries. (See Chapter 7.)

F. Preparing Your Will

As mentioned, most people can safely prepare their wills without hiring a lawyer. Let's look realistically at what's usually involved when you prepare a will. The core transaction is probably quite simple. You know who you want to get your property. There's nothing very complicated about your desires. Indeed, many people can declare in a sentence or two what they want.

Example 1: *"I want all my property to go to my husband, Arnold Kramer, or, if he dies before I do, to be divided equally between my three children."*

Example 2: *"I want my house and all my other property to go to my sister Charlotte. If she dies before me, I want all my property to go to her son, Bill. If he too dies before me, I want my property sold and the money divided equally between The Red Cross, the Audubon Society, CARE and St. Stephen's College."*

Example 3: *"I want half of my property to go to my husband Bill Tarver and the other half divided equally between my children Christopher Reilly and Mona Reilly Jamison."*

Why should turning such straightforward desires into a valid legal document be a matter for expensive estate planning experts, or any lawyer at all? It is astounding that our legal system—perhaps lawyers' culture is a more apt phrase—has steeped us in the belief that any action regarding your property and who gets it at your death is so complicated that you dare not proceed without paying a lawyer. It's as if you were required to see a doctor to take aspirin.

Despite the fulminations of some lawyers, writing a basic will is not akin to creating a new computer, building a house from scratch or (the inevitable) "brain surgery." Sure, you need useful information and carefully prepared sample forms, but (as I've surely driven home by now), it's easy to get these. Some readers will decide they need or want a lawyer. But the important thing is not to fret over the technicalities of documents like your will. Work out what you want and then see if you really need professional help.

G. Challenges to Your Will

The fact that many people worry about the possibility of lawsuits over their wills demonstrates how fear-ridden estate planning has become. Fortunately, the reality is that will challenges, let alone successful ones, are rare.

The legal grounds for contesting a will are limited to extreme circumstances. Your will can be invalidated only if you were under age when you made it, or were clearly mentally incompetent (not of "sound mind"), or the will was procured by fraud, duress or undue influence. The courts presume that the willmaker was of sound mind; a challenger must prove incapacity. Similarly, to establish fraud, duress or undue influence, someone must prove that an evildoer manipulated the willmaker, who was in a confused or weakened mental or emotional state, so that the willmaker left property in a way that she or he otherwise wouldn't have.

If You Fear a Lawsuit. *If you think someone might contest your will, it's best to see a lawyer who can help you prepare in advance how to prevail against a lawsuit. It's also prudent to see an attorney if there are special circumstances that might raise questions about your competence, such as a seriously debilitating illness. This may mean having the lawyer come to see and perhaps even physically help you. For example, in many states, if you're too ill to sign your own name, you can direct that a witness or an attorney sign it for you. If someone later claims that because you were too ill to sign your name, you weren't mentally competent to make your will, the lawyer's testimony that you appeared to be in full possession of your faculties could be very important.* ■

CHAPTER 5

Living Trusts

A living trust allows you to do the same basic job as a will—that is, leave your property to the beneficiaries you choose—with the major plus of avoiding probate. Formally, a living trust is a legal document (normally, just a few pieces of paper) that controls the transfer of property in the trust after you die. In the trust, you name beneficiaries to receive the trust property. As with a will, you name primary beneficiaries for specific property, residuary beneficiaries, and alternates for both.

Living trusts are the most popular method for transferring property outside of probate. They are very flexible. You can transfer all your property by living trust, or if appropriate, use one to transfer only some assets, leaving the rest by other methods.

Another plus is that living trusts are rarely made public after the trustmaker's death. Wills, on the other hand, become part of the public record during the probate process.

Living trusts are called "living" because they're created while you are alive; you legally transfer property to the trust when you create it. And they're called "revocable" because you can revoke or change them at any time, for any reason, before you die. While you live, you still effectively own all property you've transferred to your living trust and can do what you want with that property, including selling it, spending it or giving it away. And don't let the word "trust" scare you. We're not talking about some monstrous monopolistic tool, but a simple device that millions of savvy Americans have successfully used.

Aside from some paperwork necessary to establish a living trust and transfer property to it, there are no serious drawbacks or risks involved in creating or maintaining it. Unlike other trusts, you don't need to obtain a taxpayer ID number for the trust or maintain separate trust tax records. All transactions which are technically made by the living trust are reported on your personal income tax return.

A living trust can work as effectively for a couple as for a single person. With a couple, each member can create his or her own separate trust. More commonly, though, a couple creates one shared living trust to handle both their shared ownership property and any either owns individually. Because most couples who use living trusts are married, the discussion that follows uses the terms "spouses" and "marital property." However, the concepts discussed apply equally to unmarried couples.

A. How a Living Trust Works

Here are the basics of how a living trust works. In the trust document, you name:

- the property placed in the trust
- the trustee, who has authority to manage the trust property (you name yourself as the initial trustee; if you establish a shared trust, you and your spouse are the initial trustees)
- the successor trustee, who will to distribute the property when you die
- the trust beneficiaries, who will receive the property you've left them when you die, and
- other terms of the trust, including the fact that you can amend or revoke it at any time.

Then you formally transfer property into the trust's name. When you die, your successor trustee simply obtains the property from whoever holds it, and transfers it to your beneficiaries. No probate or other court proceeding is required.

DEFINITIONS: LIVING TRUST TERMS

The person who sets up a living trust (that's you) is called the "grantor." (Other legal terms include "trustor" and "settlor.") If you establish a shared living trust with your spouse, you are both grantors. The grantor creates a written "trust document" (or "instrument"), containing all the terms and provisions of the trust.

The property you transfer to the trustee, acting for the trust, is called, collectively, the "trust property", "trust principal" or "trust estate." (And, of course, there's a Latin version: the trust "corpus," meaning the "body" of the trust.)

To place property in your trust, you must formally transfer the property's title to the trust. If the trust does not become the official legal owner of property, that property is never validly included the trust, and so can't be transferred by it when you die. Instead, that property will go to the residuary beneficiary of your will—and through probate.

With any property having a document of title, such as a house, you must prepare a new ownership document—with a house, this means making a new deed. Technically, you transfer ownership into your name as trustee. For example, to transfer my house into my living trust, I would prepare a deed, stating that I personally transferred the house to "Denis Clifford, as trustee of the Denis Clifford Living Trust." If required, the document must be filed with the appropriate governmental agency. For example, you file a real estate deed with the County Recorder's Office—or whatever the official land records office is called in your state.

Some types of valuable property, such as jewelry or art works, as well as items like household possessions or clothes, don't normally have documents of title. In that case, the property is transferred to the living trust simply by listing it in the trust document, and stating that the property is owned by the trust.

The magic of the living trust is that, although it is really only a legal fiction during your life, it assumes a very real presence for a brief period after your death. When you die, the living trust can no longer be revoked or altered. And because property held in a living trust does not need to go through probate, the successor trustee can immediately transfer that property to the trust beneficiaries

Some paperwork is necessary to complete the transfers, such as preparing new ownership documents. Still, the successor trustee can normally handle these matters (without a lawyer) in no more than a few weeks. Once the trust property is legally received by the beneficiaries, the trust ceases to exist.

Example: *Travis wants to leave his valuable sculpture collection and his house to his daughter, Bianca, but he wants to keep complete control over the house and the collection until he dies. He also doesn't want the $300,000 value of the house and the $250,000 value of the collection to be subject to probate. Travis reasons that it's pretty silly to pay thousands of dollars in probate fees just to have his own house and sculpture turned over to his daughter after he dies.*

Travis establishes a living trust, with the house and sculpture as the trust's assets. He names himself as the initial trustee. Bianca is named as both the successor trustee and the trust beneficiary. Travis prepares and records a deed listing himself as the owner of the property, as trustee of his trust. The sculpture has no documents of tile, so it is effectively transferred to the trust by simply listing it as an asset in the trust document.

When Travis dies, Bianca takes possession of the sculpture. As trustee, she prepares and records a deed transferring the house from the trust—technically, from herself, as successor trustee of the trust— to herself, personally. The trust then ceases to exist.

Preparing your living trust documents is discussed in more detail in Section G, below.

B. Do You Need a Living Trust?

Most people who plan their estates eventually turn to a living trust to transfer some, and often the bulk, of their property. Still, not everyone needs one. Before getting deeper into a discussion of the particulars of living trusts, let's look at whether you really need one, at least for the time being. You may not want a living trust if:

You are young and healthy. The primary estate planning goals of most people in their 30s, 40s, and sometimes even older, are that their property be distributed as they want in the highly unlikely event they die suddenly, and that any young children are cared for. A will, perhaps coupled with life insurance, generally achieves these goals more easily than does a living trust. Many younger people decide to go with a will now, and prepare a living trust later in life when the prospect of death is more imminent.

You can more sensibly transfer assets by other probate-avoidance devices. Living trusts aren't the only game in town: "pay-on-death" bank accounts, joint tenancy and life insurance are among the other methods that might work better for you, at least for some of your property. (See Chapter 6.)

You have, or may have, complex debt problems. If you have many creditors when you die, probate provides an absolute cut-off time for creditors to file claims against your estate. If, after being notified, they don't do so in the time permitted, your will beneficiaries can take your property free of concern that these creditors will surface later and claim a share. A living trust doesn't create any such cut-off period.

There's no one you trust to oversee your trust after your death. You need someone you fully trust to serve as successor trustee for your living trust. No court or government agency makes sure your successor trustee complies with the terms of your living trust. If you can't name a spouse, child, other relative, friend or someone else you believe is truly trustworthy, a living trust isn't for you.

You own little property. If your property isn't worth much, monetarily speaking, probate will be unnecessary or relatively inexpensive. There isn't much point in bothering with a living trust and probate avoidance.

For all this, the fact remains that most people who plan their estates are older, and are concerned with probate avoidance. For them, a living trust usually works just fine. I'm a big fan of living trusts, having seen them help many inheritors—family, friends and clients—to receive inherited property promptly and without cost.

BE WARY OF "FREE" LIVING TRUST SEMINARS OR HIGH-PRESSURE SALESPEOPLE

There are quite a number of ads these days for free seminars on living trusts. Usually, these events are nothing more than elaborate pitches for paying a lawyer (or some non-lawyer entity or service) $1,000 or more to write a living trust. Sometimes salespeople contact prospective customers by phone and pressure them to make an appointment to buy a living trust. Is it worth it? Almost always, no.

Seminar sponsors often try to sell the idea that much of your estate is likely to be gobbled up by estate tax and probate unless you set up trusts now to avoid some of the tax and buy life insurance to pay the rest. In truth, most people don't have estates large enough to owe estate tax. (See Chapter 8.) Further, there are many ways to avoid probate, and you should evaluate them all before deciding what's best for you.

The sponsors won't tell you this, but instead hustle:
- lots of life insurance, to pay for supposed estate tax, and
- a fill-in-the-blanks trust that they claim will avoid probate while reducing estate tax—a version of what I call an AB trust. (See Chapter 9, Section B.)

Be sure you need these alleged benefits before paying a substantial amount for them. Do you really want to bother with probate avoidance now? If so, can you prepare your living trust yourself? Is your estate really likely to be liable for estate tax? If so, and you are married, does an AB trust makes sense for you? Again, with proper resources, can you prepare an AB trust yourself? You have alternatives that are likely to work better, and cost less, than buying a living trust from a seminar, which is a bit like buying aluminum siding from a door-to-door salesperson.

C. Living Trusts and Taxes

A probate-avoidance living trust has no effect on your taxes, either your income taxes while you live or estate tax when you die. (See Chapter 8 for a discussion of estate tax; the great majority of estates are not liable for any estate tax.) If you're looking for ways to avoid or lower taxes, or protect your assets from creditors, you are looking for something different than a living trust.

1. Income Tax

During your life, your living trust doesn't have a separate existence for income tax purposes. The IRS treats the trust property as it does any other property you own. Because the trust isn't functionally distinct from you while you are alive, it can't be used to lower your income tax.

SELLING YOUR HOME FROM A TRUST: TAX BREAKS

Many people put their homes—their most expensive asset—into their living trusts. If you do, you won't lose any tax benefits:

- You can still deduct mortgage interest.
- You can sell your principal home once every two years and exclude $250,000 of capital gains from income taxation. A couple can exclude $500,000.

2. Estate Tax

Let me state this in capital letters: LIVING TRUSTS DON'T SAVE ON ESTATE TAX. I emphasize this because when some people hear the word "trust," they feel it must mean "tax savings" (or "tax scam").

A probate-avoidance living trust can, however, be combined with other types of trusts that are designed to save on estate tax. A common example of this is combining an AB trust with a living trust. (See Chapter 9, Section B.) But by itself, a living trust is designed to avoid probate, and that's all. Which is plenty.

D. Living Trusts and Young Children

You can leave property to minors using a living trust. For instance, many married people name their spouse as beneficiary of their trust, and their minor children as alternate beneficiaries. If you leave property in your trust to minors, whether as direct or alternate beneficiaries, you should use the trust document to impose adult management of that property. You accomplish this by creating a child's trust, family pot trust, or by leaving a gift using your state's UTMA. (Methods for leaving property to young children are discussed in detail in Chapter 3, Section C.)

E. Shared Living Trusts for Couples

The fact that a couple can create a shared living trust covering the property of both doesn't mean they must. In some circumstances, it may make sense for each spouse to create an individual living trust. For example, if each spouse owns mostly separate property, a combined living trust may make little sense. But if spouses share ownership of much or all of their property, as is usually the case, it's generally preferable to use just one living trust for their property.

If you live in a community property state, in which spouses equally own most property acquired after marriage, you and your spouse almost certainly own property together. (To remind you, community property states are Arizona, California, Idaho, New Mexico, Nevada, Texas,

Washington, Wisconsin and, if the couple makes a written agreement, Alaska.)

Even in the other (common law) states, where one spouse may technically be the sole legal owner of much property, spouses who have been married for many years typically regard most or all property as owned by both. If so, you can transfer that property into legal co-ownership when creating your shared living trust.

Unmarried couples can also share ownership of property, if they choose, and register any ownership/title document in both their names as co-owners.

Setting up two separate living trusts for shared property owned by a couple is generally undesirable because ownership of the shared property must then be divided into two separate halves. That's a lot of trouble, and can cause ongoing record-keeping burdens. Worse, it can lead to unfair and undesired imbalances—for example, one spouse's stocks might go up in value while the other's decline. Fortunately, there is no need for spouses to divide property this way. With a shared trust, you can transfer all co-owned property to it. You can also put individually owned or separate property into the trust, and keep it separate. Each spouse has full power to name beneficiaries for his or her portion of the shared trust property, and all of his or her separate property.

When one spouse dies, the shared living trust splits into two trusts. One trust contains all property of the deceased spouse. The other contains all property of the surviving spouse. The deceased spouse's property is transferred by the successor trustee to the beneficiaries named by that spouse. Commonly the surviving spouse is a beneficiary, but children, friends and organizations may also inherit property. The diagram below shows how a shared living trust works. In this example, the husband and wife transfer their property, all shared ownership, into the trust. The husband is the first spouse to die, the "deceased spouse." The wife is the "surviving spouse."

HOW A SHARED LIVING TRUST WORKS

1. Husband and wife transfer shared property to trust.
2. Husband dies. Shared trust property is divided in half.
3. Husband's one-half ownership of shared property goes to his beneficiaries. All property owned by wife, including her half of shared property and any property left her by the deceased spouse, is transferred to her living trust.
4. Wife's property remains in her ongoing living trust.

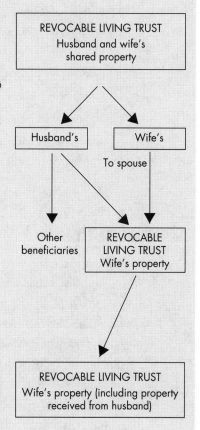

F. Making Key Decisions About Your Living Trust

Here, we'll look deeper into the four important decisions you must make
if you want to create a living trust:

1. What property will be in the trust?
2. Who will be the successor trustee? (As I've stressed, you, or you
   and your spouse, will be the initial trustee(s).)
3. Who will be your beneficiaries?
4. If you transfer most or much of the value of your estate by living
   trust, how will any debts and taxes outstanding at your death be
   paid?

1. Choosing Property to Put in the Living Trust

You can place some or all of your property in your living trust, or
transfer it by other means, such as pay-on-death accounts, joint tenancy,
or even a will. In general, if you decide to use a living trust, it's sensible
to transfer all your big-ticket items to it, unless they are covered by
another probate-avoidance technique. Property to consider includes
your home, securities accounts (stocks and bonds), investment property
and other valuable items such as jewelry or artworks.

A couple of special concerns may arise when real estate is involved:

Property taxes. In some states, transferring real estate to a new
owner can result in an immediate reappraisal of the property for property tax purposes. By contrast, if the property is not transferred to new
owners, it usually won't be reappraised for a set period of years, or (in a
few states) at all. Because you and your living trust are considered the
same basic entity while you're alive, there's no real change in ownership
and therefore no reappraisal. To be absolutely sure that this is true in
your state and county, check with your local property-tax collector.

Homestead protection. State homestead protections, which typically protect your home-equity interest from creditors up to a designated amount, should not be lost because real estate is transferred to a living trust. If you are not seriously in debt, there is no need to worry about this one. However, if you're in debt and concerned that a creditor may try to force a sale of your house, check your state's homestead rules carefully.

Other Property. You can also transfer items of lesser (or no) value by means of a living trust. A trust can be particularly useful for transferring clothes, photographs, family records, household furnishings, sports equipment or similar possessions.

There are a couple of types of property that you generally won't want to transfer by living trust: vehicles and personal checking accounts. With vehicles, insurance companies can cause problems. Most are unwilling to insure vehicles owned by a trust, maintaining that they can't determine who authorized drivers are. With your personal checking account, it's mostly a matter of style. To many people, it seems odd to pay bills with checks from a trust. Also, merchants and other businesses, especially those that don't know you well, may be wary of accepting a check in a form so out of the ordinary.

2. Choosing the Trustees of Your Living Trust

You must make two choices when it comes to naming a trustee to manage the property in your living trust: who will be the initial trustee, and who will take over as the successor trustee when the first trustee dies or becomes incapacitated.

a. Your Initial Trustee

To repeat it, you, or you and your spouse, are the initial trustee(s). If you set up a shared trust, when one spouse dies, the other continues as sole trustee. Serving as trustee is how you continue to have absolute control of your trust property.

You are not legally required to be the trustee of your trust. Occasionally, people consider naming someone else to serve as initial trustee, because they don't want to, or cannot, continue to manage their own assets. But having someone else serve as sole initial trustee makes managing your living trust more complicated. Under IRS rules, separate trust records must be maintained, and a trust tax return filed if you aren't a trustee of your living trust.

Naming Someone Else As Sole Initial Trustee. *If you want to name someone besides yourself to be your initial trustee, see a lawyer. You'll probably need much more detailed controls on the trustee's powers.*

b. Naming Co-Trustees

If you want, you can name two people (or even more) to serve as initial trustees. You might do this if you want or need someone else to manage the trust property for you while you live but you don't want the IRS complications that come with an independent trustee. You name yourself and someone else as trustees and authorize either to act for the trust. Because you are, legally, one of the trustees, the IRS does not require you to keep separate trust records or file a trust tax return.

c. Your Successor Trustee

As you know by now, it's essential that you name at least one successor trustee for your living trust. Your successor trustee is the person who makes your trust work after you die. With a shared trust, the successor trustee takes over after both spouses die. Also, the successor trustee is normally authorized to take over management of the trust if you (or you and your spouse, with a shared marital trust) become unable to handle it yourself.

You should also name an alternate successor trustee, in case the successor trustee dies before you do or for any other reason can't serve.

d. The Job of the Successor Trustee

The primary job of the successor trustee is to turn trust property over to the beneficiaries you've named in your trust. Because no court approval is required, this task is normally not difficult—as long as the property and beneficiaries are clearly identified in the trust document. Still, some effort is required. The successor trustee must know where the trust property is located. For any property held by an institution, such as banks or stock brokerage companies, the trustee must get the cooperation of the institution to turn over that property to the beneficiaries. Institutions that deal with financial assets are familiar with living trusts and how they work. They should not balk at accepting the authority of the successor trustee.

The successor trustee also prepares any new documents of title necessary to turn trust property over to the beneficiaries.

In addition to dealing with property subject to formal ownership (title) documents, the trustee supervises the distribution of all other trust assets—household furnishings, jewelry, heirlooms, collectibles—to the appropriate beneficiaries. The trust ends when all beneficiaries have actually received the trust property left to them in the trust document.

e. Choosing Your Successor Trustee

Your successor trustee should be trustworthy, and willing and able to do the job. Normally, this is the same person you choose as the executor of your will. (See Chapter 4, Section B.) Similarly, your alternate successor trustee is normally the person you choose for your successor executor.

Often a principal beneficiary, such as a spouse or adult child, is named as successor trustee. However, if you believe the beneficiary (much as you love him or her) will be troubled by the practical details and paperwork, it's better to name someone else.

You can name co-successor trustees. Indeed, you can name as many successor trustees as you want, with power divided between them as you specify. However, because of problems coordinating trust management tasks and possible conflicts, it's risky to name multiple trustees. On the other hand, sometimes there are compelling reasons to do so.

For example, you might name two or more children as successor co-trustees, to avoid being seen as favoring one child over others. But be sure all co-successor trustees get along well. If there's any risk of conflict, naming co-successor trustees is a bad idea.

Finally, don't name a bank or financial institution as successor trustee if you can possibly avoid it. I've heard plenty of horror stories involving the indifference or downright rapaciousness of banks acting as trustees of family living trusts. But if there is no human being you believe will act honestly and competently as your successor trustee, and after reviewing the other probate-avoidance devices discussed in this book, you are still determined to establish a living trust, you'll need to select some financial institution to do the job. Probably the best choice here is a private trust company.

3. Naming Your Trust Beneficiaries

You can leave each beneficiary whatever trust property you want, with one big exception. In common law states (see the list in Chapter 2, Section A) a married person may be required to leave a certain percentage of the trust estate—usually one-half—to the other spouse. However, in some common law states, the spousal inheritance protection laws apply only to property left by will, not by living trust. Also, in almost all common law states, a spouse can waive his or her spousal inheritance rights.

Leaving Your Spouse Less Than Half of Your Trust Property in a Common Law State. *If you want to leave your spouse less than half of your trust property, see a lawyer to make sure you don't run afoul of your state's spousal inheritance protection law.*

Aside from any applicable spousal protection law, with a shared trust you and your spouse can each choose your own trust beneficiaries. You may want to name your spouse as your sole primary beneficiary. Or you may want to divide your gifts between several people or institutions.

Example: *Malcolm and Ursula, married for 30 years, create a shared living trust. They have one child, Suzanne. Each spouse leaves the bulk of his or her property to the other. Each also leaves some smaller gifts to different relatives, friends and charities. Both name Suzanne as their alternate beneficiary and residuary beneficiary. Ursula names Suzanne's husband, Tom, as her alternate residuary beneficiary. Malcolm names his niece Martha as his alternate residuary beneficiary.*

4. Arranging for Payment of Debts and Taxes

Many people don't leave any substantial debt or tax obligations when they die. (Leaving a house with a mortgage isn't a concern here: the mortgage simply passes with the house.) If you have only routine bills at your death, your successor trustee and executor will pay them, either from property you earmarked in your trust or will for this purpose, or from trust or will property generally. Either way, no beneficiary will suffer a substantial loss. If you fit into this category, you can go on to other concerns. If, however you transfer the bulk of your property by living trust and will likely have significant debts, including estate tax, it's best to identify trust assets that should be used to pay off these obligations. First, of course, you'll need to make a realistic appraisal (or at least a decent guess) of what you'll owe, for both regular debts and taxes, at your death.

LIVING TRUSTS AND YOUR DEBTS

Property in a revocable living trust is not immune from attack by your creditors while you're alive. You have complete and exclusive power over the trust property, so a judge is not going to let you use the living trust (which you can revoke at any time) to evade creditors. On the other hand, if you place property in a trust that you can't revoke or change (called an "irrevocable trust"), it's a different legal matter. Your creditors cannot reach property owned by a bona fide irrevocable trust. The key words here are "bona fide." If an irrevocable trust is set up only to defraud creditors, it won't work.

Some "authorities" have inaccurately stated that property in a revocable living trust can't be grabbed by your creditors during your life. They argue that, for collection purposes, a revocable living trust is legally distinct from its creator. I know of no law or case that supports this position.

 Shielding Your Assets. If you're concerned about protecting your assets from creditors, see a lawyer.

G. Preparing Your Living Trust Documents

Now we'll take a closer look at what you actually do when you prepare a living trust.

1. The Trust Document

No law specifies the form a living trust must take. As a result, there is no such thing as a standard living trust. Indeed, there are a bewildering variety of living trust forms, including some attorney-created forms that contain vast piles of verbiage that serve little real-world purpose, except to generate attorney fees.

You most likely want something simpler. Aside from naming your trustee, successor trustee and beneficiaries, your trust document contains all other provisions governing the trust. This includes identifying the trust property, usually by listing the property on one or more "schedules" attached to the main trust document. You need only identify each item of property with sufficient clarity so that your successor trustee and beneficiaries unambiguously know what you meant. No legal rules require property to be listed in any particular form. For example, you can list property generally as "all my ballroom gowns," or "all household possessions at ... (address)" or "all my books."

You must sign the trust document in front of a notary public. Unlike wills, no witnesses are required.

2. Transferring Property Into Your Trust

For purposes of transferring title into the trust there are two types of property: property that has ownership (title) documents and property that doesn't.

a. Property Without Ownership Documents

Many types of property don't have title documents, including all kinds of household possessions and furnishings, clothing, jewelry, furs, tools, most farm equipment, antiques, electronic and computer equipment, art works, bearer bonds, cash, precious metals and collectibles. You transfer these items to your trust simply by listing them on a trust schedule. In addition, you can use a "Notice of Assignment" form, a simple document that states that the property listed on it has been transferred to the trustee's name.

b. Property With Ownership Documents

To make your trust effective, it is absolutely essential that you transfer ownership of property with documents of title into your trust—technically, to you as trustee. If you fail to do this properly, your successor trustee won't be able to transfer that property to your beneficiaries.

Property with title documents includes:

- real estate, including condominiums and cooperatives
- bank accounts
- stocks and stock accounts
- most bonds, including U.S. Government Securities
- corporations, limited partnerships and partnerships
- money market accounts
- mutual funds
- safe deposit boxes

- vehicles, including cars, most boats, motor homes and planes.

On the new documents of title you formally list the trustee of the trust as the new owner. For example, if Ellen Yurok wants to place her house into her trust, she prepares a deed, listing herself (individually) as the person transferring title, and the new owner as "Ellen Yurok, as trustee for the Ellen Yurok Trust." (After the trust name, many lawyers add "u/t/d/" or "under trust dated" and then list the date the trust was signed and notarized.) With a shared trust, both people's names are used. Thus, Helen and Marshall Fink transfer a home from themselves to "Helen and Marshall Fink, as trustees of the Helen and Marshall Fink Trust."

You then must file this document as is appropriate for that type of property. With a real estate deed, you file and record it with your local land records office. With a stock market account, you give the new account form to the brokerage company. With a boat registered with the Coast Guard, you complete the appropriate Coast Guard forms (they have them) and file them with that agency.

Many estate planning lawyers insist on preparing and recording all documents transferring title to trust assets. Generally, they don't necessarily do it to raise their fees (though that is one result) but because they believe that clients can't be relied upon to do the job right. I think that with clear instructional materials you can do this work yourself. But even if you end up letting a lawyer do the work, you'll benefit from gaining a basic understanding of what it involves.

If you name your living trust itself as the beneficiary of property, you do not have to re-register title to that property. For example, if you want your living trust to receive the proceeds of your life insurance, which will then go into a family pot trust, you do not register the trust as the owner of the policy. It is not the owner. You remain the owner until you die. The trust is simply who you've named, in the insurance policy, to receive benefits payable on your death. ■

CHAPTER 6

Other Probate Avoidance Methods

Aside from a living trust, there are a number of other probate-avoidance methods. You can mix and match these methods, using the ones that work best for you.

You might wonder why you should bother with anything but a living trust, when it seems to work so well. The answer is that in certain situations other methods are easier to use, while providing the same probate-avoidance benefits. For instance, a simple pay-on-death bank registration is usually a better way to handle your checking account than a living trust.

In this chapter, we'll look beyond the living trust to other probate-avoidance methods, except for using an individual retirement plan for probate avoidance, which is covered in Chapter 7.

A. Pay-on-Death Bank Accounts

Setting up a pay-on-death bank account—sometimes called an informal bank account trust, revocable trust account, or Totten trust—is an easy way to transfer cash at your death, quickly and without probate. All you do is designate, on a form provided by the bank, one or more persons you want to receive any money in the account when you die.

You can do this for any kind of bank account, including savings, checking or certificate of deposit accounts. And banks don't charge more for keeping your money this way. When you die, the beneficiary claims the money simply by showing the bank the death certificate and personal identification.

Example: *Thérèse opens a savings account in her name, and names Lynn Zelly as the pay-on-death (P.O.D.) beneficiary. When Thérèse dies, any money in the account will go directly to Lynn.*

There are no risks in creating a P.O.D. bank account. During your life, the beneficiary has absolutely no right to the money in the account. You can withdraw some or all of the money, close the account or change the beneficiary at any time.

Like other bank accounts, a P.O.D. account may be temporarily frozen at your death if your state levies estate tax. The state will release the money to your beneficiaries when shown that your estate has sufficient funds to pay the taxes.

Before you open a P.O.D. account, ask your bank if there are any special state law requirements about notifying the beneficiary. In a few states, a P.O.D. provision isn't effective unless you have notified the beneficiary that you've set up the account. Your bank should be able to fill you in on your state's rules.

You can also register ownership of certain kinds of government financial obligations, such as bonds, Treasury bills and Treasury notes, in a P.O.D. form. However, you can name only one beneficiary for these securities.

B. Transfer-on-Death Accounts for Securities

In states that have adopted the Uniform Transfers-on-Death Security Registration Act, you can add a transfer-on-death designation to individual securities (stocks and bonds) or securities accounts. Security accounts are broker-held accounts for your stocks, bonds, mutual funds or similar investments.

STATES THAT ALLOW TRANSFER-ON-DEATH REGISTRATION OF SECURITIES

Alabama	Nebraska
Alaska	Nevada
Arizona	New Hampshire
Arkansas	New Jersey
California	New Mexico
Colorado	North Dakota
Connecticut	Ohio
Delaware	Oklahoma
Florida	Oregon
Idaho	Pennsylvania
Illinois	South Dakota
Iowa	Tennessee
Kansas	Texas
Maryland	Utah
Minnesota	Virginia
Missouri	Washington
Mississippi	West Virginia
Missouri	Wisconsin
Montana	Wyoming

The beneficiary or beneficiaries you designate will receive these securities promptly after your death. No probate is necessary.

Your broker should have a form that allows you to use transfer-on-death registration for a securities account. For individual stock or bond certificates, contact the company's transfer agent.

⚠ Your Broker Isn't Required to Cooperate. *Although most stock brokers and corporate transfer agents offer transfer-on-death registration where legally permitted, the law doesn't require them to do so; it simply allows them that option. Of course, if they don't offer you the opportunity, you can threaten to switch brokers, or sell your shares, which may well overcome resistance.*

C. Transfer-on-Death Car Registration

Presently, only two states allow vehicles to be registered in a transfer-on-death form. Missouri pioneered using car registration as a probate-avoidance device and California adopted a similar law. (A few years after it was adopted, however, some local California DMV offices had not heard of it and had no forms for it. The California law, in case you need to convince a skeptical clerk at the DMV, is Section 4150.7 of the Vehicle Code.)

Under the Missouri law, a car owner can use the vehicle title document to designate a person or persons to receive ownership of the car when the present owner dies. The new owners obtain title to the car (and the car itself) without any court proceedings. California law is similar, except that California allows this method for only one owner (not for co-owned cars) and you can name only one beneficiary.

> ### AVOIDING PROBATE FOR BOATS
>
> In some states, such as California, transfer-on-death registration is available for small boats, called "undocumented vessels," which include the myriad of small pleasure boats that aren't required to have a valid marine document from the U.S. Bureau of Customs. In California, only one owner and one beneficiary may be listed (California Vehicle Code Section 9852.7).

D. Joint Tenancy

In the right circumstances, joint tenancy can be a very handy probate-avoidance device. The key to deciding whether you want to use it for some of your property is to see if your needs fit within those circumstances.

1. How Joint Tenancy Works

Joint tenancy is a form of shared property ownership. For estate planning purposes, the most important characteristic of joint tenancy is that when one owner (called a joint tenant) dies, the surviving joint owner or owners automatically inherit the deceased owner's share. This is called the "right of survivorship." The property doesn't go through probate. There is some simple paperwork which must be completed to transfer the property into the name of the surviving owner(s), but this can be easily done.

By contrast, other forms of shared ownership, such as "tenancy in common," or corporate or partnership interests, do not create a right of survivorship.

 State Law Restrictions on Joint Tenancy. *In Alaska and Tennessee, joint tenancy is not allowed, except for husband and wife.*

Joint tenancy is most commonly used for real estate, though it is legally available for all types of property.

Example: *Evelyn and Joe own a house in joint tenancy. Evelyn dies. Joe, because of his "right of survivorship" inherits Evelyn's share of the house, outside of probate. Joe is now the sole owner of the house.*

A joint tenant cannot leave his or her share to anyone other than the surviving joint tenants. So even if Evelyn, in the previous example, had a will leaving her half-interest in the house to her son, her husband would still get her ownership of it.

In addition, all joint tenants must own equal shares of the property. If you want unequal ownership portions, joint tenancy is not for you.

Joint tenancy certainly has the virtue of simplicity. To create a joint tenancy, all new co-owners need to do is pay attention to the way they are listed on the document that shows ownership of property, such as a deed to real estate, a car's title slip or a card establishing a bank account. In the great majority of states, by calling themselves "joint tenants with the right of survivorship," the owners create a joint tenancy. In a few states, additional specific words are necessary.

Wording for a Joint Tenancy. *If you want to set up a joint tenancy and aren't sure how to word a title document in your state, ask a lawyer or, for real estate, someone at a land title company.*

A joint tenant can, while still alive, break the joint tenancy by transferring his or her interest in the property to someone else—or, in most states, to himself, but not as a "joint tenant." The new owner is no longer joint tenant, but owns her share of the property as a "tenant in common." Indeed, once one owner transfers her share of property out of joint tenancy, that joint tenancy is destroyed for all owners, and they all become tenants in common.

SIMULTANEOUS DEATH OF JOINT TENANTS

Many joint tenants are concerned about what will happen to their property if they die simultaneously. After all, if there's no surviving owner, the right of survivorship that's central to joint tenancy has no meaning. To deal with this highly unlikely but still potentially worrisome possibility, in your will you can name a beneficiary to inherit your share of joint tenancy property in the event that all owners die simultaneously. If you don't do this, and all the owners die simultaneously, your share will pass under your will to your residuary beneficiary.

---

2. When to Consider Joint Tenancy—And When to Avoid It

To generalize and simplify a bit, joint tenancy can be desirable for people who buy property and want to share ownership, including inheritance rights. By contrast, it is rarely sensible for a sole owner to transfer property into joint tenancy with another simply to avoid probate of that property. Doing this creates several problems that don't occur when you pass your property using a living trust:

You can't change your mind. If you make someone else a joint tenancy owner of property that you now own yourself, you give up half-ownership of the property. The new owner has rights that you can't take back. For example, the new owner can sell or mortgage his or her share. And even if the other joint tenant's half isn't mortgaged, it could still be lost to creditors.

Example: *Maureen, a widow, signs a deed that puts her house into joint tenancy with her son to avoid probate at her death. Later, the son's business fails, and his creditors sue him. Those creditors can take his half-interest in the house to pay the court judgment, which means that the house might be sold. Maureen would get the value of her half in cash; her son's half of the proceeds would go to pay the creditors.*

By contrast, if you put property in a living trust, you don't give up any ownership now. You are always free to change your mind about who will get the property at your death. And your beneficiaries' creditors cannot reach the property as long as you remain alive.

There's no way to handle the incapacity of one joint tenant. If one joint tenant becomes incapacitated and cannot make decisions about the property, the other owners must get legal authority to sell it or obtain a mortgage. That may mean going to court to get someone (called a conservator, in most states) appointed to manage the incapacitated person's affairs.

With a living trust, if you (the grantor) become incapacitated, the successor trustee (or the other spouse, if it's a shared trust) takes over and has full authority to manage the trust property. No court proceedings are necessary.

Gift tax may be assessed. If you create a joint tenancy by making another person a co-owner, federal gift tax may be assessed on the transfer. If you give gifts to one person (except your spouse) exceeding $10,000 in any calendar year, you must file a gift tax return with the IRS. (See Chapter 8, Section C.) There's one exception: If two or more people open a bank account in joint tenancy, but one person deposits all or most of the money, no gift tax is assessed against that person. A taxable gift may be made, however, when a joint tenant who has contributed little or nothing to the account withdraws money from it.

A surviving spouse could miss a tax break. If you make your spouse a joint tenant with you on property you previously owned individually, your spouse could miss out on a potentially big income tax break later, if the property is sold.

With joint tenancy property, the Internal Revenue Service rule is that a surviving spouse gets what's called a "stepped-up tax basis" for only the half of the property owned by the deceased spouse. (Basis means the dollar number from which taxable profit or loss is calculated when property is sold. See Chapter 8, Section D for a discussion of stepped-up basis.) By contrast, if you leave your solely owned property to your spouse through your living trust or will, the entire property gets a stepped-up tax basis.

E. Tenancy by the Entirety

"Tenancy by the entirety" is a form of property ownership that is similar to joint tenancy, but is limited to married couples. It is available only in the states listed below.

STATES THAT ALLOW TENANCY BY THE ENTIRETY

Alaska*	Maryland	Ohio
Arkansas	Massachusetts	Oklahoma
Delaware	Michigan*	Oregon*
District of Columbia	Mississippi	Pennsylvania
Florida	Missouri	Rhode Island
Hawaii	Tennessee	
Illinois	New Jersey*	Vermont
Indiana*	New York*	Virginia*
Kentucky*	North Carolina*	Wyoming*

*Allowed for real estate only.

Tenancy by the entirety has almost the same advantages and disadvantages of joint tenancy and is most useful in the same kind of situation: when a married couple acquires property together. When one spouse dies, the surviving spouse inherits the property without probate.

If property is held in tenancy by the entirety, neither spouse can transfer his or her half of the property alone, either while alive or by will or trust. A living spouse must get the other spouse's consent to transfer the property; at death, it must go to the surviving spouse. (This is different from joint tenancy; a joint tenant is free to transfer his or her share to someone else during his life.)

Example: *Fred and Ethel hold title to their apartment building in tenancy by the entirety. If Fred wanted to sell or give away his half-interest in the building, he could not do so without Ethel's signature on the deed.*

Property held in tenancy by the entirety is better protected from the creditors of either spouse than is joint tenancy property from creditors of any owner. In most states, if someone sues one spouse and wins a court judgment, the creditor can't seize and sell the tenancy-by-the-entirety property to pay off the debt. (Obviously, if a creditor proves both spouses are liable for a debt, he can go after the couple's shared-ownership property, including tenancy-by-the-entirety property.) And if one spouse files for bankruptcy, creditors cannot reach or sever the property held in tenancy by the entirety.

F. Community Property With Right of Survivorship

Married couples in one of these four community property states—Arizona, Nevada, Texas, Wisconsin—have another option that may be useful. Couples in Arizona, Nevada, or Wisconsin can hold title to their community property "with right of survivorship"—meaning that when one spouse dies, the other automatically owns all the property. Texas lets couples make a written agreement that some or all of their community property will have a right of survivorship.

These arrangements offer all the benefits of community property ownership, plus the important advantage that the property doesn't go through probate when one spouse dies. Instead, the surviving spouse owns it automatically.

Wisconsin law goes even further. It lets married couples avoid probate altogether for their marital property. In a "marital property agreement," they can name as beneficiary any person, organization or trust to inherit their marital property, without probate. And like an AB trust (discussed in Chapter 9, Section B), the agreement can even provide for the disposition of marital property at the death of both spouses. Unlike an AB trust, however, after the first spouse dies, the survivor may amend the agreement unless the agreement itself expressly forbids it.

G. Simplified Probate Proceedings

Many states have begun, albeit slowly, to dismantle some of the more onerous aspects of probate. As discussed in Chapter 4, Section D, most states have some form of simplified probate. What qualifies as a small estate varies from state to state, from $5,000 or less in some states to $140,000 in Oregon.

For small estates, many states require only an affidavit procedure. By filling out a sworn statement (the affidavit) and giving it to the person who holds the property, inheritors can collect property left them by will. The beneficiary must also provide proof of his or her right to inherit, such as a death certificate and copy of the will.

H. Life Insurance

As life insurance agents will be delighted to explain, life insurance is a good way to provide surviving family members with quick cash for debts, living expenses and, for larger estates, estate taxes. And because you name the beneficiary in the policy itself, not in your will, life insurance proceeds don't go through probate.

CHOOSING LIFE INSURANCE

If you're thinking about purchasing life insurance, you may feel overwhelmed by the bewildering array of policies available to you. Despite the various and confusing names for different kinds of life insurance, there are basically two types to consider for estate planning purposes: term insurance or "permanent" insurance (commonly called "whole life" or "universal" insurance). Term life insurance, the least expensive type, provides insurance for a set period. For example, a five-year $150,000 policy pays the entire amount if you die within five years—and that's it. Term insurance is particularly well suited to younger parents. As a candid life insurance agent once told me, "It provides the most bang for the buck, no question." However, once the term has expired, you have to reapply to get new life insurance. By contrast, permanent insurance is automatically renewable. You cannot be required to take a new physical exam. With a permanent policy, your premium payments for the years cover more than the actuarial risk of your death. The insurance company invests the excess money, and a portion of the returns is passed along to you.

For more information and help deciding which type of life insurance policy is best for you, consult *Consumer Reports Life Insurance Handbook: How to Buy the Right Life Insurance Policy at the Right Price* (Consumer Reports Books).

The only circumstance in which life insurance proceeds are subject to probate is if the beneficiary named in the policy is your estate. That's done occasionally if the estate will need immediate cash to pay debts and taxes, but it's usually counterproductive. It's almost always a better idea to name your spouse, children or another beneficiary who can take the money free of probate and use it to pay debts and taxes.

Although the proceeds of a life insurance policy don't go through probate, they are included in your estate for federal estate tax purposes if the person who died was the legal owner of the policy. If you think your estate might be liable for federal estate taxes, you can reduce the tax bill by giving away the policy to the beneficiary, another person or an irrevocable life insurance trust. (See Chapter 8, Section C and Chapter 9, Section C.)

I. Gifts

Here's a surprise: If you give away property while you're alive, there will be less property in your estate to go through probate when you die. While in theory you could avoid probate by giving away all your property, common sense dictates using one or more of the methods discussed previously, which let you keep control over your property while you're alive.

Making gifts of up to $10,000 per calendar year per person, however, may be a good strategy if you expect your estate to owe federal estate tax after your death, and you want to reduce the eventual tax bite. (See Chapter 9, Section A.) ■

CHAPTER 7

Retirement Plans As Estate Planning Devices

Retirement plans, which may compose a big part of your savings, can function as estate planning devices. In particular, if you have an individual retirement program such as an IRA, 401(k) or Profit-Sharing Plan, these can hold significant amounts of money if you die prematurely. Any money left in a retirement account is part of your estate. With any individual retirement program, you should name one or more beneficiaries to receive any money left in the account when you die. The money goes directly to your beneficiaries, and is not subject to probate.

Before we look further into how you can use your retirement plans in estate planning, it's important to note that these devices are not intended to provide money to beneficiaries. They are designed to provide money to you, the owner, in your retirement. Because of this, federal law requires that after you reach age 70½ you must withdraw at least a certain portion of your retirement account every year or face a monetary penalty. (Roth IRAs function differently. See Section A.2, below.) The withdrawal amount is recalculated every year, based on your current life expectancy and, to some extent, that of your beneficiary. So if you live to a ripe old age, there will be no or very little money left in your account when you die. Thus, for estate planning purposes, these accounts are not fixed assets, like a house, that you can reasonably count on to retain (at least) their full present value.

Information on Retirement Planning. *When they retire, most people are entitled to payments from one or more retirement programs, such as Social Security, military benefits, private or public employee pensions, union pension plans or individual retirement accounts. Planning for a financially comfortable retirement can be complicated, and I don't pretend to address that subject here. There are numerous books, magazines, websites and proclaimed experts who can give you all the advice you may want, and then some. Here are some good resources available from Nolo.*
Get a Life: You Don't Need a Million to Retire, *by Ralph Warner*

Beat the Nursing Home Trap, *by Joseph Matthews*

Tax Savvy for Small Business, *by Frederick W. Daily.*
You can also visit Nolo's website at www.nolo.com to learn more about planning for retirement.

A. Individual Retirement Programs

In addition to Social Security, savings and investments, many people contribute regularly to one or more individual retirement programs that will assure them an income when they get older.

1. Traditional Individual Retirement Programs

As you doubtless know, individual retirement programs such as regular IRAs (Individual Retirement Accounts), Profit-Sharing Plans (formerly called Keogh plans) and SEP-IRAs (IRAs for the self-employed) are retirement plans you fund yourself. The money you contribute is tax deductible, within limits. You are in charge of how the money is invested. You don't pay tax on any earnings, either, in the year earned. After you retire, when you withdraw money from the account, that money is taxable income in the year you get it.

Profit-Sharing Plans and SEP-IRAs are for the self-employed. By contrast, any income earner can create a regular IRA by making annual contributions. Currently, annual contributions to a regular IRA of up to $2,000 are tax deductible if you aren't covered by a company retirement plan. This deduction is phased out for high earners. The contribution limit for a Profit-Sharing Plan or a SEP-IRA is a percentage of net income, and can be well over $2,000.

More Information About Individual Retirement Programs. *IRS Publication 590 provides detailed (and complex) information on personal retirement arrangements, such as IRAs. IRS Publication 560 covers retirement plans for the self-employed, such as Profit Sharing Plans. You can download these publications for free by visiting the IRS's website at www.irs.ustreas.gov.*

2. Roth IRAs

The Roth IRA, a new kind of individual retirement account, differs from the traditional IRA in several respects. You fund a Roth IRA with up to $2,000 per year that has already been taxed. (By contrast, the money you place in a regular IRA is tax deductible in the year contributed.) All earnings from money in a Roth IRA are tax-free. And when you withdraw money, no further income tax is due, as long as the money was in the account for at least five years.

The biggest difference, for estate planning purposes, between regular IRAs (and most other retirement plans) and a Roth IRA is that you don't have to start withdrawing money from a Roth IRA when you reach age 70½. So, if you choose, you can leave all of a Roth IRA untouched when you die—and this money will pass to your named beneficiary, free of probate.

3. 401(k) or 403(b) Plans

Many employers now offer employees what are called 401(k) plans and 403(b) plans. (The 401(k) is for businesses, the 403(b) for nonprofit corporations.) Employees can, if they choose, defer a portion of their pre-tax wages, having them paid instead into the retirement plan. Many employers match these funds or at least make some contribution to the account.

Money in your account is invested, growing (well, you hope it grows) tax-free until you withdraw it. As with an IRA, you must begin withdrawing money from the account at age 70½, based on your life expectancy. The amount you must withdraw is recalculated every year. At your death, the beneficiary you've named receives whatever funds are left in the account, without probate. If you are married, the beneficiary must be your surviving spouse unless your spouse signed an agreement giving up this right. (See Section C, below.)

B. Pensions

A pension, unlike an individual retirement program, is not under your control. Your company sets up a pension plan and determines what rights you receive. You may acquire the right to receive payments— perhaps generous ones—and this right may extend to your spouse after you die. But what you have are rights to benefits, not ownership of assets as you have with an individual retirement program. Beyond any rights that may extend to your surviving spouse, you have no right to pass your benefits to beneficiaries—unless the pension plan authorizes this, which very few do.

No law requires an employer to offer a pension plan. And there's no legal requirement that a pension plan pay benefits to a surviving spouse. Some are generous; some provide nothing after the employee dies.

More Information About Pension Plans. *IRS Publication 575 discusses the rules for many pension plans, but it's not easy reading. You can download it for free from the IRS website at www.irs.ustreas.gov. A number of brochures on pensions, which are easier to understand, are available from The American Association of Retired Persons (AARP), 601 E Street NW, Washington, DC 20049, 800-424-3410, www.aarp.org, and The Pension Rights Center, 918 16th Street NW, Suite 704, Washington, DC 20006, 202-296-3778.*

C. Choosing Beneficiaries for Individual Retirement Programs

If you have an individual retirement program, it may contain a substantial amount of money when you die. Choosing who will inherit any remaining funds may be one of the most important estate planning decisions you make.

You should always name a beneficiary for an individual retirement program, such as an IRA, Roth IRA, Profit-Sharing or 401(k) plan. You can name more than one beneficiary if you like. Indeed, you can name many beneficiaries, with any money left in the account divided between them as you specify, and name alternate beneficiaries for each primary beneficiary.

There's one big exception to your freedom to name beneficiaries. You **must** name your spouse as sole beneficiary of your 401(k) or 403(b) program, unless your spouse waives that right. This can become an important, and sensitive, matter.

Example: *Arlette is in her mid-40s, has a well-paying job in computer graphics, and a 14-year-old daughter. Arlette's one major asset is a chunk of money in her company's 401(k) program. Long divorced, Arlette wants to marry Adam. But she does not want him to be the beneficiary of her 401(k) program; she wants the beneficiary to continue to be her daughter. It may require some tact for Arlette to successfully explain to her fiancé why she's asking him to sign a waiver of rights shortly before the marriage.*

Also, in community property states, each spouse has a legal half-interest in money that the other spouse has earned during the marriage, unless that spouse signs a document giving up the interest. (This waiver is accomplished in a separate document from that which waives 401(k) inheritance rights.)

In reality, many married people do name their spouses as the beneficiaries of their individual retirement program. They want to support their spouses, and for larger estates, defer possible estate tax. (Leaving assets to the surviving spouse postpones tax, under the marital deduction, until the death of that spouse. See Chapter 8, Section C.) But as long as you don't run afoul of laws requiring retirement program money to be left to a spouse, you can name anyone you want as beneficiary. For one reason or another, some people do name a child or other person as beneficiary.

D. Retirement Plans and Taxes

All money you leave in an individual retirement program—for example, the remaining balance in an IRA, Roth IRA or 401(k) plan—is subject to federal estate tax when you die. It doesn't matter how the funds are paid out, whether in a lump sum or over time. The dollar value of the account at death is part of your estate for estate-tax purposes. Whether tax will have to be paid depends on the net value of your entire estate, and the year of death. (See Chapter 8, Section A.)

Also, the beneficiary will have to pay income tax on any money left in most retirement plans. (This is not the case with most other inherited assets.) These payments are due because when the money was first socked away, the contributions were tax deductible, as was any money the account earned. Now that the money is withdrawn, the taxman wants his cut, regardless of the death of the person who created the account. However, a surviving spouse may be able to "roll over" money from a deceased spouse's IRA into her own IRA, and not have the money subject to income tax until she makes withdrawals from her account.

Money in a Roth IRA is not subject to income tax when the beneficiary inherits it. That's because money contributed to a Roth IRA is taxed when made; the IRS has already taken its bite. Also, any earnings from contributions that have been in the account for at least five years are not taxed when withdrawn by the inheritor. However, money earned in the account after the initial depositor's death is subject to income tax. ■

Estate Tax

Before you plunge into the subject of estate tax, you should know that most people don't have to worry about it. Most estates are too small to be taxed. (Is this good or bad news?) Basically, no federal estate tax is assessed if the net value of your taxable estate at death is less than $650,000 to $1 million, depending on the year of death.

On the other hand, if you are quite prosperous, federal estate tax can take a large bite out of your estate. The tax rate is determined by the size of the taxable estate; the more you own, the higher the rate. The tax rate starts at 37% and rises to 55% for estates over $3 million.

In addition, a minority of states impose estate tax (sometimes called inheritance tax or death tax) on the property of a deceased person who lived or owned real estate in that state. But when estate planners talk about estate tax, the focus is almost always on federal tax, which can devour much more of an estate than can state taxes.

NO INCOME TAX ON INHERITED PROPERTY

Because many people worry about this, I want to state explicitly that people who inherit property do not have to pay income or capital gains tax on the worth of the property. (One exception is funds in most individual retirement accounts; see Chapter 7, Section D.) However, after a person inherits property, any income subsequently received from the property is regular income, and is subject to income tax.

A. Federal Estate Tax Exemptions

Several federal tax law exemptions and deductions allow you to leave substantial amounts of property free of estate tax. The most important of these are:

The personal exemption. This allows you to leave a total of $650,000 to $1 million free of tax, no matter to whom you leave the property. (See Section A.1, below.)

The marital deduction. This exempts from tax all property, no matter how much it's worth, left by a deceased spouse to a surviving spouse. (See Section A.2.) However, if the surviving spouse is not a citizen of the U.S., the marital deduction does not apply.

The charitable deduction. This exempts all property left to a tax-exempt charity. (See Section A.3.)

The small business exemption. This is a special exemption for estates worth up to $1.3 million, where the majority of the estate is a qualifying family business. (See Section A.4.)

In addition, certain types of property do not have to be valued at their "best use" market value for federal estate tax purposes. These include family farmland and wooded land. So even if farmland would be worth far more if sold to a developer to build an apartment complex or a shopping center, you don't have to use that higher value. Further, your estate can have up to 14 years to pay off estate tax on a closely held business, including a family farm, if the value of your estate's interest in it exceeds 35% of the total value of the estate.

1. The Personal Estate Tax Exemption

This exemption relieves the great majority of estates from federal tax. Each year, a set dollar amount of property is exempt from tax, no matter to whom the property is left. The chart below sets out the yearly exemptions.

THE PERSONAL ESTATE TAX EXEMPTION

Year of Death	Amount of Personal Exemption
1999	$650,000
2000-2001	$675,000
2002-2003	$700,000
2004	$850,000
2005	$950,000
2006 and after	$1,000,000

I use the term "estate tax threshold" to mean the amount of the personal exemption in a given year. For example, the estate tax threshold for 2001 is $675,000; for 2005 it is $950,000.

If you have made taxable gifts during your life, the amount of the personal exemption will be reduced accordingly. Currently, you can give property worth up to $10,000 per recipient in a calendar year free of tax. (See Section C, below.)

Example: *Cerita gives Max $110,000 in 1999. $10,000 of the gift is exempt from gift tax. The remaining $100,000 will be deducted from her personal estate tax exemption. Cerita dies in 2004, when the estate tax threshold is $850,000. Her personal exemption is $750,000.*

2. Property You Leave to Your Spouse

As stated earlier, all property you leave to your U.S. citizen spouse is exempt from federal estate tax. In tax lingo, this is called the "marital deduction."

Example: *Pamela leaves $3 million to her husband Rinaldo. No estate tax is assessed.*

You must be legally married to qualify for the marital deduction. There are no similar exemptions for mates, "significant others" or lovers.

The marital deduction works in addition to all other allowable estate tax deductions.

Example: *Marty has an estate valued at $4.1 million. He leaves $600,000 to his children and the rest, $3.5 million, to his wife. All Marty's property is exempt from federal estate tax—the $3.5 million because of the marital deduction and the $600,000 because it is below the estate tax threshold.*

a. How the Marital Deduction Can Be a Tax Trap

The fact that no federal estate tax is assessed when property is left to the surviving spouse may mislead prosperous couples into thinking that leaving everything outright to each other is always the best thing to do, tax-wise. Often it is not, from an estate tax standpoint. The marital deduction can have a downside if a couple owns assets worth more than the estate tax threshold, and each leaves everything to the other. The result, increasing the size of the surviving spouse's estate, might lead to an estate tax bill when there otherwise would be none, or higher estate tax.

Example: *Pauline and Judah are married and own all their property together. Each one's share is worth $650,000. If Judah dies first, leaving all his property to anyone but Pauline, his estate won't owe tax because its value is under the estate tax threshold. If Judah leaves everything to Pauline, no tax will be due* *because of the marital deduction. However, if Pauline later dies with an estate worth $1.3 million (her $650,000 plus her inheritance of $650,000), tax must be paid. Somewhere between $650,000 and $1 million of her property will be exempt, depending on the year of her death, but a minimum of $300,000 will be subject to tax. If Pauline owns only her half of their original estate, her estate won't owe any tax at all.*

This tax trap is particularly severe when both spouses are elderly. The survivor isn't likely to live long enough to benefit much from outright ownership of the deceased spouse's property. It is often wiser, from an estate tax viewpoint, to use the personal exemptions of both members of the couple, rather than only one, as can occur if the marital deduction is used.

The standard way to avoid the marital deduction tax trap is to create what's called an AB trust, where each spouse places all or most of his property in the trust. The surviving spouse normally has the rights to all income from trust property, use of the trust property (such as the right to continue living in the couple's home), and can even spend the principal for essential reasons like healthcare costs, but he or she never becomes the legal owner of the trust property. (See Chapter 9, Section B, for further discussion of how an AB trust works.)

b. Special Rules for Non-Citizen Spouses

As I've said, no marital deduction is allowed for property left by one spouse to a spouse who is not a citizen of the United States. It doesn't matter that a non-citizen spouse was married to a U.S. citizen or is a legal resident of the U.S. The surviving spouse must be a U.S. citizen to be eligible for the marital deduction. (On the other hand, property a non-citizen spouse leaves to a citizen spouse is eligible for the marital deduction.)

Why this discrimination against non-citizen spouses? Congress feared that non-citizen spouses would leave the U.S. after the death of their citizen spouses, whisking away their wealth to foreign lands, so it would never be subject to U.S. tax.

Fortunately, you can still leave your non-citizen spouse a good deal of property free of estate tax. The personal estate tax exemption can be used for property left to a non-citizen spouse, as well as to anyone else. So property worth between $650,000 and $1 million (to say it again, depending on the year of death) can be left tax-free to a non-citizen spouse.

Example: *Lacey leaves all her property to her husband Pascal, a non-citizen. When she prepares her estate plan, her estate is worth $500,000. Whatever the year of her death, this amount will be under the estate tax threshold. However, in 2002, Lacey unexpectedly inherits $400,000 and dies shortly thereafter. Her total estate is worth $900,000. The personal estate tax exemption for 2002 is $700,000. Because Pascal is not a citizen, $200,000 of Lacey's estate is subject to tax.*

Congress provided one way that a spouse can leave property to a non-citizen spouse and obtain additional estate tax protection. Property left to a non-citizen spouse in what's called a "Qualified Domestic Trust" (or "QDOT") is allowed the marital deduction.

Example: *Giuseppe is married to Dominique, a non-citizen. Giuseppe dies with an estate of $2 million. He leaves $600,000 to his son, and $1.4 million to Dominique in a QDOT trust. No taxes are due when he dies. The property in the QDOT trust qualifies for the marital deduction, and the $600,000 is not taxed because it is under the estate tax threshold.*

Creating a QDOT Trust. *To prepare one of these trusts, you'll need a lawyer. QDOT trusts are tricky, and you need to understand all the estate tax consequences, including the fact that your property will eventually be taxed on its worth when your spouse dies, as part of that estate, not what it is worth when you die, as part of your estate.*

3. Gifts to Charities

All gifts you leave to tax-exempt charitable organizations are exempt from federal tax.

If you are wealthy, you may want to explore a "charitable remainder trust" for making gifts to charities. With a charitable remainder trust, you make a gift to a charity while you live, and then receive a certain annual income from the gift property during your life—either a fixed dollar amount or a fixed percentage of the annual net worth of the gift asset. There are income tax, as well as estate tax, benefits that flow from a charitable remainder trust. (Gifts to charities are further discussed in Chapter 9, Section C.)

4. Estate Tax Rules for Family Businesses

Special federal rules may allow you to avoid estate tax when you leave a family business as part of an estate worth more than the estate tax threshold. For a qualifying family business, a total estate of $1.3 million can be transferred free of tax, no matter what the year of death. Because it's highly unlikely that an estate will consist only of a family business, some of this total exemption will apply to other property. But if the entire estate is solely a family business, that business can be worth up to $1.3 million without incurring estate tax.

The $1.3 million exemption combines the personal estate tax exemption in the year of death and an additional family business tax exemption to reach the total, as shown in the chart below.

THE COMBINED PERSONAL AND FAMILY BUSINESS EXEMPTIONS

The total exemption is always $1,300,000. Here's a breakdown of the numbers from year to year.

Year	Personal Exemption	Family Business Exemption
1998	$625,000	$675,000
1999	$650,000	$650,000
2000-2001	$675,000	$625,000
2002-2003	$700,000	$600,000
2004	$850,000	$450,000
2005	$950,000	$350,000
2006 and after	$1,000,000	$300,000

The family business exemption law contains a number of requirements designed to ensure that it is not abused. Your business must meet each of the following requirements to qualify for the exemption.

Inheritors. All inheritors must be family members, or employees who have worked in the business for at least ten years. After the primary owner's death, these inheritors must continue to participate in the business for at least five years out of any eight-year period during the ten years following the deceased owner's death.

Ownership. 50% of the business must be owned by one family, or 70% by two or 90% by three. If more than one family owns the business, the family seeking the business exemption must own at least 30% of the business.

Business Value. The value of the business must exceed 50% of the total value of the deceased person's estate.

Disposal of Interest. If an inheritor disposes of his or her interest in the business, or ceases to materially participate in it, the IRS recaptures the estate tax that would have been due at the deceased person's death. If the inheritor disposes of the interest within the first six years, the entire amount of the estate tax on that interest must be paid. In years seven through ten, the amount of the tax is based on a declining scale.

Using the Family Business Exemption. *The family business exemption is new and complicated. If you think it might apply to you, see a lawyer.*

B. State Death Tax

Twenty-seven states and the District of Columbia have effectively abolished state death tax. The rest impose tax on:

- all real estate owned in the state, no matter where the deceased person lived, and
- all property of residents of the state, no matter where it's located.

In most states that have it, this tax is called an inheritance tax. In a few, it is called estate tax. Although theoretically different—one's a tax on the person who inherits, the other a tax on the estate itself—the reality is the same. The tax is paid from the deceased person's property.

STATES WITH, EFFECTIVELY, NO DEATH TAX

"Effectively" there is no death tax in the following states because, in all but Nevada, there is something called a "pick-up" tax. This tax is simply a way of shifting some money that would otherwise be paid in federal estate tax to the state. So the estate pays the same total tax that it would if there were no pick-up tax. However, the pick-up tax does mean that a state death tax return must be filed for estates over the estate tax threshold.

Nevada is the only state that has abolished all death tax, and thus the only state where a death tax return never need be filed, no matter how large the estate.

Alabama	Illinois	South Carolina
Alaska	Maine	Texas
Arizona	Minnesota	Utah
Arkansas	Missouri	Vermont
California	Nevada	Virginia
Colorado	New Mexico	Washington
District of Columbia	North Dakota	West Virginia
Florida	Oregon	Wisconsin
Georgia	Rhode Island	Wyoming
Hawaii		

State Tax Rules. *Death tax rules for all states are summarized in* Plan Your Estate, *by Denis Clifford and Cora Jordan (Nolo). More detailed information is available from state tax officials.*

C. Gift Tax

The federal government imposes a tax on substantial gifts made during life. This tax came about because Congress reasoned that if only property left at death were taxed, people would give away as much property as they could during their lives, effectively voiding the estate tax laws. So gift tax rates are the same as estate tax rates, to eliminate any tax incentive for making large gifts. The tax is imposed on the giver of the gift, not the recipient.

If you make a taxable gift, you do not actually pay any tax at that time. Indeed, under IRS rules, you are not permitted to pay the tax at that time. Instead, the amount of the taxable gift must be deducted from your estate tax exemption.

Example: *Jerry gives Hamid a gift, $60,000 of which is subject to gift tax. Jerry cannot choose to pay the tax on that amount now. Instead, the $60,000 will be deducted from the amount of his personal estate tax exemption when he dies. Jerry dies in 2003, when the personal exemption is $700,000, so his personal exemption is $640,000.*

There are several important exceptions to the gift tax rules: the annual exemption, the marital exemption and an exemption for gifts to cover medical bills or school expenses. In this section, I'll discuss each in turn.

1. The Annual Exemption

Federal law exempts (technically, it's called an "exclusion") a set dollar value of gifts from tax. Currently, you can give up to $10,000 per calendar year per person free of gift tax.

Example: *Suno gives each of her five children $10,000 in 1999. All of these gifts are tax exempt.*

Both members of a couple have separate $10,000 exemptions, so they can give a combined total of $20,000 per person per year tax free.

Example: *In 2000, Elliot and Gina give $20,000 to their daughter, $20,000 more to her husband, and $20,000 to each of their daughter's three children. All these gifts are tax exempt.*

As this example shows, over time, wealthy people can give away large amounts of money tax free. Elliot and Gina gave away $100,000 in one year. Multiply that sum by, say, five years, and you get an idea of just how much can be removed from a wealthy estate by an extensive gift-giving program.

The $10,000 gift tax exemption is indexed yearly to the cost of living. As the cost of living rises (assuming it does, which seems a safe bet) the gift tax exemption will also rise, in increments of $1,000 rounded down to the lower thousand. In other words, cost of living increases must cumulatively raise the current exemption by more than $1,000 before the gift tax exemption is raised to $11,000.

2. The Marital Exemption

All gifts between spouses are exempt from gift tax, no matter how much the gift property is worth. This rule is part of the marital deduction discussed above in Section A.2.

The marital deduction does not apply to gifts from a citizen spouse to a non-citizen spouse. The rule here is that gifts worth up to $100,000 per year can be made to a non-citizen spouse, tax free. Thus, a citizen spouse with an estate worth $900,000 can be sure that his estate won't owe tax if he gives his non-citizen spouse $100,000 in each of three years; his remaining estate of $600,000 is under the estate tax threshold.

3. Gifts for Medical Bills or School Tuition

If you pay someone else's medical bills or school tuition, your gift is tax exempt. This exemption has a couple of twists, however. First, you must pay the money directly to the provider of the medical service or the school. If you give the money to an ill person or student, who then pays the bill, the gift is not tax exempt. Nor can you reimburse someone who has already paid a medical or tuition bill and receive the tax exemption. Finally, you cannot get the exemption for payments covering a student's other educational expenses, such as room and board.

D. The Federal Income-Tax Basis of Inherited Property

Though it's not, strictly speaking, an estate tax matter, the question of how inherited property is valued for the purpose of calculating gain or loss from a subsequent sale is closely related, and important to many people. Generally, if you own property that has significantly increased in value since you bought it, it's desirable from a tax standpoint to leave that property to others when you die, rather than to sell it or give it away during your life. To understand why this is so, we have to take a little jaunt into tax land.

Let's start with a definition. The word "basis" means the value assigned to property from which taxable gain or loss on sale is determined. The concept of a property's basis is a tricky one, not made any easier by the fact that "basis" is not defined in the tax laws. When property is purchased, its basis is generally its cost. In fact, basis is often referred to as "cost basis." For example, if you buy some stock for $5,000 it has a basis equal to its cost—$5,000. If you sell the stock two months later for $16,000 (lucky you), your taxable profit is $11,000.

Sale Price	$16,000
Minus Basis	- $5,000
Taxable Gain	$11,000

The original cost basis can be adjusted up, for certain types of improvements to property, or down, for reasons like depreciation. For instance, if you make what's called a "capital improvement" to a house, such as putting in a new foundation, the cost of the improvement is added to the basis of the property. A capital improvement can be very roughly defined as an improvement that lasts more than a year.

Example: *Green Is Good, Inc., buys an old barn in which to design and make bicycles. The barn costs the company $270,000, so it has a cost basis of $270,000. Over the next year, Green Is Good spends $230,000 for capital improvements to the barn, installing a new fire-control system and a new roof. Here's how the company determines the adjusted basis:*

Original Cost	*$270,000*
Plus Capital Improvements	*+ $230,000*
Adjusted Basis	*$500,000*

On its income tax return, the company takes depreciation deductions of $30,000 for the barn. The property's adjusted basis is now $470,000, because the deduction for depreciation lowers the adjusted basis of the property.

After several years, Green Is Good needs a larger production plant. It sells the barn for $700,000 to The Mogul Company, which plans to convert the barn into rental apartments for skiers.

Green Is Good determines its profit this way:

Sale Price	*$700,000*
Minus Basis	*- $470,000*
Taxable Profit	*$230,000*

The Mogul Company's basis in the barn is $700,000.

Now to move to the tax basis of inherited property. Under federal tax law, the basis of inherited property is "stepped-up" to its fair market value at the date of the deceased owner's death. Actually, this is a simplification of the rule, which is that the basis of inherited property is adjusted *up or down* to the market value as of the date of death. However, the assumption that prices of property rise over time is so ingrained in our economic life that the term commonly used is "stepped-up" basis. And in practice, for property owned for a long period of time, the inheritor's basis—the net value of the property at death of the previous owner—is almost always higher than that of the previous owner.

Example: *The Mogul Company is solely owned by I. B. Wily. In five years of ownership, he spent $350,000 turning the barn into apartments, and took $150,000 total depreciation. His basis in the building is calculated as follows:*

Purchase Price	*$700,000*
Plus Capital Improvements	*+ $350,000*
Minus Depreciation	*- $150,000*
Adjusted Basis	*$900,000*

After his fifth year of ownership, Mr. Wily dies, leaving the building to his daughter, Ursula. At his death, the building is valued at $1.5 million. Ursula's basis in the building is "stepped-up" to this $1.5 million.

The fact that the basis of property is stepped up to its fair market value at the owner's death means that it's almost always desirable to hold on to appreciated property until it can pass at death. That way, your inheritors obtain the advantage of the stepped-up basis rule. Thus, if Wiley sold the building for $1.5 million shortly before he died, he would have had to pay federal capital gains taxes (and probably state income taxes) on $600,000 ($1.5 million sale price minus his $900,000 basis). By contrast, if Ursula sells the building for $1.5 million, no tax will be assessed.

Gifts made during life are not entitled to a stepped-up basis. Only transfers at death qualify for this desirable tax treatment. So if Wily gave the property to his daughter a few weeks before he died, her basis would be $900,000.

THE TAX BASIS OF JOINT TENANCY PROPERTY

With joint tenancy property, only the portion owned by the deceased owner gets a stepped-up basis. The portion owned by surviving joint tenants continues to have the same basis it had before.

Example: Colette and Marion buy an apartment house in joint tenancy, each contributing half the purchase price of $400,000. Each person's share has a basis of $200,000. Five years later, Colette dies, and the apartment house has a net value of $800,000. The basis of Colette's half interest in the property is stepped up to $400,000 from $200,000. But Marion's share retains it's basis of $200,000.

Because the property was owned in joint tenancy, Marion, of course, receives Colette's share. Here is Marion's basis in the property:

Marion's Share	$200,000
Colette's Share	+ $400,000
Net Basis	$600,000

Two years later, Marion sells the apartment house for $850,000. Here is Marion's profit, for capital gains tax purposes:

Sale Price	$850,000
Minus Marion's Basis	- $600,000
Profit	$250,000

CHAPTER 9

Reducing Federal Estate Taxes

What can you do to reduce federal estate taxes if you think your estate will be liable for them? Not as much as you might hope. Of course, for the very wealthy, high-priced experts do come up with ingenious, or twisted, ways to dodge taxes. For the rest of us, aside from making use of the estate tax exemptions and deductions discussed in Chapter 8, there are basically only two ways to reduce estate tax: make gifts during your life, or set up what's called an irrevocable trust. That is, a trust that cannot be changed after it goes into effect, in contrast to a living trust, which can be amended or revoked as long as you are alive.

A. Making Gifts During Life

Obviously, if you give away property while you live, that removes the value of that property from your taxable estate. Here we'll look at different types of gifts you may want to make.

1. Using the Federal Gift Tax Exclusion

As you know from the discussion in Chapter 8, you can make gifts worth up to $10,000 per person per calendar year free of gift tax. A couple can give $20,000 per year tax-free to any person. Tax-exempt gift giving can remove large amounts of money from an estate. A gift-giving program can be particularly advantageous for wealthy folks who have several children, grandchildren or other people they'd like to help.

You can also make tax-free gifts of any amount for:

- payments made for someone's educational or medical costs, and
- contributions to tax-exempt charities. If you're quite prosperous, you may want to look into what's called a "charitable remainder trust."

The rules for reducing your estate by making these types of tax-free gifts are discussed further in Chapter 8, Section C.

2. Gifts of Interests in a Family Business

Gifts of minority interests in a family business can, in the right circumstances, reduce estate taxes. This is because a minority interest can be valued, for gift tax purposes, at less than the value it would have if it were part of the majority interest.

Example: *Angela gives her daughter Lucia 10% of Angela's interest in her furniture company. At the time of the gift, the company is worth $1 million. The value put on Lucia's 10% share is not $100,000, but something significantly less, in the $60,000 to $80,000 range, because of minority business discounts. (The accounting rules here are fuzzy, and a tax professional must be consulted.)*

While this method can be helpful for an existing business, it's unlikely to work if you try to create a business and place your major assets, such as your home, in it. Under IRS rules, a family business must serve a valid business purpose and cannot be designed solely or primarily to reduce estate taxes.

Some "experts" have touted one particular business form, called a "family limited partnership," as a wonderful device for eliminating estate taxes. There's nothing at all magical about this type of business. It cannot transmute non-business assets into a valid family business.

Reducing Taxes on a Family Business. *If you have a family business and believe your estate may be liable for estate tax, see a lawyer to learn your options for reducing the tax bite. Be sure to find out whether your estate will be eligible for the family business estate tax exemption. (See Chapter 8, Section A.4.)*

3. Gifts of Life Insurance

From an estate tax standpoint, it can be very desirable to give away life insurance during your life. If you own your life insurance policy at your death, the proceeds (death payment) are included in your taxable estate. If the policy has a large death benefit—say, hundreds of thousands of dollars—including that sum in your taxable estate can result in substantial federal estate taxes. But the proceeds will not be subject to tax if someone else owns the policy when you die.

> ⚠️ **Don't Wait to Make a Gift of Life Insurance.** *Under IRS regulations, a gift of life insurance must be made at least three years before your death. The potential tax savings from making a gift of life insurance are so large that the IRS will not allow any "death-bed" gifts. Defining "last minute" to mean at least three years does seem a tad excessive, but it's pointless to quarrel with the tax folks over this one.*

Gifts of life insurance are subject to gift tax. The worth of the gift is, basically, the current value of the policy. This will always be far less than the amount the policy will pay at your death. If the present value is under $10,000, no gift tax will be assessed.

There are two ways you can transfer ownership of a life insurance policy. First, you can simply give the policy to another person or persons. Your life insurance company should have an assignment form you can use to accomplish this. Second, you can create an irrevocable life insurance trust, and transfer ownership to that entity. You'd create a trust if there's no person to whom you want to assign the policy outright. (See Section C, below, for a fuller explanation of why you might want a trust.)

Transferring ownership of your policy to another person or a trust involves a trade-off: Once the policy is transferred, you've lost all power over it, forever. You cannot cancel it or change the beneficiary. To make this point bluntly, suppose you transfer ownership of your policy to your spouse, and later get divorced. You cannot cancel the policy or recover it from your now ex-spouse. Nevertheless, in many situations, the trade-off is worth it—for example, when you transfer policy owner-ship to a child or children with whom you have a close and loving relationship.

B. The AB Trust

An AB trust allows a prosperous couple (one that has a combined estate over the estate tax threshold) to achieve substantial savings on overall estate taxes—that is, the total paid by both members.

To remind you, the personal estate tax exemption allows a set amount of property to pass free of tax. The amount depends on the year of death, as shown below.

THE PERSONAL ESTATE TAX EXEMPTION

Year of Death	Exempt Amount
1999	$650,000
2000-2001	$675,000
2002-2003	$700,000
2004	$850,000
2005	$950,000
2006 and after	$1,000,000

As discussed in Chapter 8, Section A.2, if a prosperous spouse leaves most, or all, of her property to the surviving spouse, the estate of the survivor can well rise well above the estate tax threshold.

Estate planners call the tax that is due on the death of the surviving spouse the "second tax." The result of the second tax is a reduction of the amount of money available to a couple's final inheritors, usually their children.

Example: *Sven and Nancy have a combined estate, owned equally, of $1 million. Each leaves his or her property (worth $500,000) to the other. Eventually, when the second spouse dies, they want everything to go to their child, Heidi.*

Sven dies in 1999. No estate tax is due, because his property is left to his wife. (Even if Sven left his property to someone else, no tax would be due because his estate of $500,000 is under the estate tax threshold for 1999.)

After Sven's death, Ingrid's estate is worth $1 million. It has the same value when she dies in 2002. The personal exemption for that year is $700,000. So $300,000 is subject to estate tax. This is the "second tax." The tax owed is $116,000—money Heidi doesn't get.

It is this second tax that an AB trust is designed to eliminate.

For estate tax purposes, it's desirable to keep the two spousal estates legally separate. But commonly, spouses want the other to continue to have use of their shared property after one spouse dies. They don't want to achieve estate tax savings at the cost of cutting a surviving spouse off from half of the couple's property.

Enter the AB trust, where you can have most of the best of these two worlds. With an AB trust, each spouse's estate is kept legally separate, but the surviving spouse can use the trust property, including the principal, for healthcare or other basic needs.

1. How an AB Trust Works

AB trusts are well established. They require some work to create, but generally are not very complex.

Each spouse sets up an AB trust, transferring most or all of his or her property to that trust. Spouses usually do this within one overarching living trust. As long as both spouses live, the couple's property remains in the living trust, which can be revoked or changed. What's special is that as part of the living trust, each spouse creates a separate AB trust— two trusts within the living trust. Each spouse leaves all, or at least the bulk, of his or her property to what's called Trust A, instead of leaving it outright to the survivor. (Sometimes, spouses also leave small gifts of their property outright to other beneficiaries.)

When the first spouse dies, the living trust property is split into two separate trusts: Trust A, the deceased spouse's trust, which now becomes irrevocable, and Trust B, the surviving spouse's living trust which can still be revoked

Because there is no way of knowing which spouse will die first, each spouse creates both an A and B trust. But even though both spouses must have an A trust, only one will become operational—that of the first spouse to die. The surviving spouse now has no use for his or her own A trust, since by definition there's no other spouse.

Example: *Chris and Wendy create an AB trust and transfer all of their property to it; each owns half of their $1,250,000 estate. When Chris dies in 1999, the trust divides in half. Chris' property goes into the irrevocable Trust A, which becomes operational. Wendy's property goes into the revocable Trust B. Wendy's A trust will never become operational. When she dies, the property in her B trust will be transferred to her final beneficiaries.*

When creating an AB trust, each spouse names the other as what's called the "life beneficiary" of his or her Trust A. This means that the surviving spouse can use and benefit from the Trust A property for the rest of his or her life, with certain restrictions, but does not have outright ownership of it.

The life beneficiary usually has substantial rights in the Trust A property. Specifically, under IRS rules the surviving spouse can have all of the following rights:

- to receive all income from the trust property
- to use trust property
- to spend trust principal in any amount for health, education, support or maintenance in accord with his or her accustomed manner of living.

If given this last right, the surviving spouse is permitted to spend part or even all of the trust property on what concerns most couples, particularly older couples—healthcare and other basic needs.

Each spouse also names final beneficiaries for his or her AB trust. Final beneficiaries receive all the AB trust property after the surviving spouse dies.

Every trust must have a trustee to supervise and manage trust property. With an AB trust, each spouse normally names the other as the first successor trustee. So the surviving spouse becomes both the life beneficiary and trustee of Trust A.

When the surviving spouse dies, an alternate successor trustee winds up both Trusts A and Trust B.

Example: *Continuing with Chris and Wendy's AB trust, each names the other spouse as the life beneficiary of, and successor trustee for, his or her Trust A. The life beneficiary has the maximum rights allowed by the IRS in the Trust A property: the right to receive all trust income, use trust property and spend the trust principal as needed for health costs or other basic needs. Both name their children Jacques, age 42, and Jane, age 38, as final beneficiaries, to share property equally. After Chris dies, Wendy, as successor trustee of Trust A, manages that trust's property and spends it within the limits established by* the trust document. Wendy also continues to manage the property in her revocable Trust B. When Wendy dies, Trust B becomes irrevocable. The alternate successor trustee turns the property in Trust A and Trust B over to the final beneficiaries.

2. How an AB Trust Reduces Estate Tax

Let's look closer at how an AB trust obtains estate tax savings. As you now know, the surviving spouse is not the legal owner of the Trust A property, so that property is not entitled to the marital deduction. Rather, the Trust A property is subject to estate tax when the first spouse dies. If this property is worth less than the estate tax threshold for the year of death, no federal estate tax is assessed. And when the second spouse dies, the Trust A property is not subject to tax at all.

Example: *Christine and Terry have three children and a combined estate worth $1.1 million. If each leaves his or her half ($550,000) outright to the surviving spouse, that spouse will be left with an estate of $1.1 million. An estate that large will be subject to estate tax, no matter what the year of death. The taxable amount will vary, of course, because of the gradual increase in the personal estate tax exemption until 2006. If the surviving spouse dies in 2001, when the personal exemption is $675,000, tax will be owed on $425,000. If the surviving spouse dies in 2006, when the personal exemption is $1 million, $100,000 will be subject to tax.*

Christine and Terry prepare AB trusts. Each names the other as life beneficiary and trustee of his or her Trust A, giving the maximum rights to use of Trust A property for healthcare and other basic needs. Then, each names their three children as final beneficiaries, to share equally in the Trust A and Trust B property after the second spouse dies.

Christine dies in 2000. The AB trust property is now divided into Trust A (her property) and Terry's revocable Trust B. No estate tax is due on Christine's $550,000 Trust A property, because it is well under the personal exemption of $675,000 for that year. Terry's estate is well under the estate tax threshold when he dies in 2009. At that time, the three children inherit the Trust A and Trust B property in equal shares.

Preparing Your Own AB Trust. *You can find information and forms for preparing Nolo's AB trust, which gives the surviving spouse the maximum allowable rights in Trust A property, in* Make Your Own Living Trust, *by Denis Clifford (Nolo).*

3. Is an AB Trust Right for You?

An AB trust can work well for you if:

- You want to leave all or the bulk of your estate to your spouse.
- You and your spouse have a combined estate that is likely to owe estate tax.

AB trusts can be particularly desirable for elderly and prosperous couples. If the surviving spouse is unlikely to outlive the other by many years, the survivor probably won't need to spend the trust principal. By contrast, younger spouses are often understandably reluctant to risk imposing the restrictions of an AB trust on property one spouse leaves for the other's benefit.

a. Personal Concerns

From a personal point of view, an AB trust works best when all involved—both spouses and all final beneficiaries—understand and agree on the purposes of the trust, which is to save on estate tax and at the same time give the surviving spouse maximum rights to use Trust A money and property. Without this understanding, serious conflicts may develop between the surviving spouse and the final beneficiaries. More specifically, an AB trust generally works well if:

- The final beneficiaries understand that all property in Trust A morally, albeit not legally, belongs to the surviving spouse. It is available for the survivor's basic needs, such as healthcare or other essentials.

- The final beneficiaries understand that taking the trouble to create an AB trust is a generous act by parents, who do this not to benefit themselves, but their inheritors. After all, the estate tax savings benefit only the final beneficiaries, who receive more (usually much more) of the couple's combined estate than they would if the spouses had left property outright to each other.

- Family members trust each other enough that it's reasonable to believe they can resolve any inheritance conflicts without lawsuits (or bloodshed).

- The final beneficiaries can be trusted to support the surviving spouse if he (as trustee) decides he needs to spend trust principal for reasons authorized by the IRS and listed in the trust document—that is, "support, health, education and maintenance in accord with his or her accustomed manner of living." They won't question these expenditures (if there are any) in an effort to preserve the largest possible amount for themselves.

If there is any potential for conflict between the surviving spouse and the final beneficiaries of the trust (often the couple's children), an AB trust may provoke or aggravate it. After all, in theory at least, there is an inherent conflict of interest between the life estate beneficiary and the final beneficiaries. These final beneficiaries may want all the trust principal conserved, no matter what the needs or wishes of the surviving spouse.

Another problem can arise if the surviving spouse becomes ill and can no longer serve as trustee. If a child who stands to inherit trust assets takes over as successor trustee, it's possible the child might be more concerned with preserving principal than with a parent's medical or other needs. I've heard of instances where it seemed to other family members and friends that a child, acting as trustee of Trust A, disregarded his parent's basic needs to protect the trust principal for himself.

Conflicts can also occur if the final beneficiaries believe the surviving spouse, as trustee, is not managing the Trust A property sensibly—for example, he is investing in very speculative stocks. If this situation arises, there can be real trouble, possibly even a lawsuit.

 Having Doubts? *If you have doubts about these personal matters, a conventional AB trust is probably not for you. See a lawyer to discuss your concerns.*

b. Couples Unlikely to Want an AB Trust

Some married couples facing estate tax won't want to use a conventional AB trust. First, there are couples who, for one or more reasons, don't want to leave the bulk of their property to each other. (For instance, couples in second marriages who have children from prior relationships may want to make sure that the bulk of their property goes to their children. See Chapter 10, Section A.) Also, some wealthy couples need far more extensive tax planning, though an AB trust will probably be part of their plan. (See Section C, below.) Finally, an AB trust is generally not advisable for:

Younger middle-aged couples—roughly, couples in their 40s, perhaps 50s. In this age group, you probably won't want to tie up assets in a trust that may last for many years or decades if one spouse dies prematurely. The surviving spouse could live for many years and be seriously burdened by the restrictions of the trust.

Many younger couples create a simple shared living trust to leave each other all or most of their property without probate. (See Chapter 5.) Then, once they're older—say in their late 50s or 60s—they revoke their old living trust and create a new one including an AB trust. After all, before then, if one spouse unexpectedly dies, the survivor will inherit everything estate tax free, no matter what the amount, because of the marital deduction. That surviving spouse will probably have years to use the money—and years to arrange for other methods of reducing any possible estate tax.

Couples where one spouse is considerably younger than the other and presumably will live much longer. Again, there's generally no need to burden the surviving spouse with a trust designed to reduce estate taxes when he or she is likely to live for many years. (Of course, such couples may well sensibly decide to use a simple shared living trust, to avoid probate.)

4. Drawbacks of an AB Trust

Before deciding to use an AB trust, both spouses should understand what they're getting into. After one spouse dies, that spouse's Trust A becomes irrevocable. The trust imposes limits and burdens on the survivor that cannot be changed.

Here are some possible drawbacks of an AB trust:

a. Restrictions on the Surviving Spouse's Use of the Property in Trust A

With an AB trust, the surviving spouse generally has the right to any income generated by Trust A property and fairly broad rights to use the property for health, education and support. But he cannot spend trust property freely on whatever he feels like, because except for legally permitted expenditures, that property must be held in trust for the final beneficiaries.

b. Administrative Expenses

When one spouse dies, an estate lawyer or accountant is commonly needed to determine how to best divide the couple's assets between the irrevocable Trust A and Trust B. Each item of the couple's shared property does not have to be divided 50/50 between the two trusts. The only requirement is that the value of the shared property in both trusts must be equal. This means there is considerable flexibility in allocating assets between the two trusts. Usually, it takes an expert to decide on the best division.

c. Trust Tax Returns

The surviving spouse, as trustee of Trust A, must obtain a taxpayer ID number for this trust. Also, the surviving spouse must file an annual income tax return for the trust. This usually isn't a momentous hassle but like any tax return, it will require work.

d. Recordkeeping

The surviving spouse must keep two sets of books and records, one for his own property (which remains in the surviving spouse's revocable living trust) and one for the property in Trust A, which (as you know by now) is legally separate from property owned by the surviving spouse.

Finally, to end on a note of optimism: Despite the possible drawbacks and limits, AB trusts have worked very well for many thousands of couples and families. An AB trust can work just fine for you, too, and may save your children or other final inheritors a bundle. For most surviving spouses, the drawbacks amount to no more than relatively minor accounting and recordkeeping hassles. These tasks may be well worth the effort if they save tens or even hundreds of thousands of dollars for your beneficiaries.

C. Other Tax Saving Trusts

There several types of irrevocable trusts that can be useful for wealthy couples who want to save on estate taxes.

> **Preparing an Estate Tax Saving Trust.** *An attorney must prepare any of the estate tax saving trusts discussed in this section. IRS regulations applicable to irrevocable trusts are complicated. A mistake can cost your inheritors all the tax savings you planned for, and then some. Also, irrevocable trusts are designed to function for relatively long periods of time, which means that there must be careful consideration of contingencies that may arise. Drafting such a trust is difficult. This section gives you an overview; if you want to learn more about the basics of irrevocable estate tax saving trusts before you see a lawyer, consult* Plan Your Estate, *by Denis Clifford and Cora Jordan (Nolo).*

1. The QTIP Trust for Married Couples

A QTIP ("Qualified Terminable Interest Property trust") is used to postpone, not eliminate or reduce, payment of estate tax. It is normally used when a spouse's individual estate exceeds the estate tax threshold. This means that even if the spouse sets up an AB trust, some estate tax will be due on the individual's death if all her assets go into Trust A.

Example: *Maxine has an estate worth $2 million. She leaves all her property in an AB trust. She dies in 2002, when the estate tax exemption is $700,000. $1.3 million of her estate is subject to tax.*

With an estate "overage," a spouse can postpone tax by leaving all this overage to the surviving spouse. (Remember, all property left to a surviving spouse is exempt under the marital deduction.) But a spouse may want neither to have her estate pay taxes when she dies, nor to leave any overage to the surviving spouse. Commonly, this is because she wants her property to go eventually to her children or other inheritors.

Here's where a QTIP trust can be helpful. With a QTIP, as with an AB trust, the surviving spouse must be left use of the trust property for life. But unlike an AB trust, property in the QTIP trust qualifies for the marital deduction. In other words, QTIP trust property isn't subject to tax when the spouse who created the trust dies. And also, with a QTIP, the spouse who sets it up gets to name the final beneficiaries. When the surviving spouse dies, the QTIP trust property goes to whomever the trust creator chooses to inherit it.

Example: *Maxine has recently married her fourth husband, James. She has three children from her first two marriages. In her estate plan, she leaves an amount equal to the estate tax exemption for the year of her death to be divided equally between her three children. For the balance of her property, she creates a QTIP trust, with James as the life beneficiary and her three children as the final beneficiaries. When Maxine dies in 2002, James is still alive. No estate tax is due as long as he lives.*

Estate tax is assessed on property in a QTIP trust when the surviving spouse (the life beneficiary) dies. The trust property is counted as part of the surviving spouse's estate. Here we reach the main drawback of QTIP trusts. When taxes are assessed, the property in the trust is valued at what it is worth when the surviving spouse dies, not what it was worth when the first spouse died. If the value of the trust property has significantly increased, this can mean a higher tax bill.

Example: *Maxine left property worth $1.3 million in her QTIP. James (the life beneficiary) dies in 2005, with an estate worth $800,000, plus the value of the QTIP property. In just three years, the value of the QTIP property has increased from $1.3 million to $1.9 million. The full $1.9 million is included in James' taxable estate, which thus totals $2.7 million.*

Deciding whether to use a QTIP is a complex matter. I've just scratched the surface here; using QTIPs can get much more complicated. For example, there is a "reverse QTIP election" that can be used to divide part of the property originally scheduled for a QTIP into two parts, only one of which goes into the trust. But I won't burden you with an explanation of how a reverse QTIP election works—or with the particulars of other sophisticated uses of this type of trust. If you've got a lot of money, see a good estate planning lawyer to find out whether if a QTIP is something you want.

2. Life Insurance Trusts

An irrevocable life insurance trust is a legal entity that owns life insurance you previously owned. You create a life insurance trust that becomes operational right away (while you live) and transfer your insurance policy to the trust.

Once you transfer ownership of life insurance, the trust owns the policy, not you. That means the proceeds aren't part of your estate and can't be subject to estate tax.

Why bother to create a life insurance trust, when you can remove insurance proceeds from your estate simply by giving ownership of the policy to someone else? Usually, because there's no adult to whom you want to give your policy. In other words, you want to get the proceeds out of your taxable estate, but you want to the legal control over the policy that a trust can offer. For example, the trust can specify that the policy must be kept in effect while you live, eliminating the risk that a new owner of the policy could decide to cash it in.

Example: *Judith is the divorced mother of two children in their 20s who will be her beneficiaries. Neither is sensible with money. Judith has an estate worth $500,000, plus a life insurance policy that will pay $700,000 at her death. She wants to be sure her estate will not be liable for estate tax, and so desires to transfer ownership of her policy. However, there's no one Judith trusts enough to take the policy outright. With the controls she can impose through a trust, however, she decides it's safe to allow her sister, the person she's closest* *to, to be the trustee of a life insurance trust for the policy. She creates a formal trust, and transfers ownership of the life insurance policy to that trust. After Judith's death, her sister will handle the money for the children under the terms of the trust document.*

There are strict requirements governing life insurance trusts. If you want to gain the estate tax savings:

- The life insurance trust must be irrevocable. If you retain the right to revoke the trust, you will be considered the owner of the policy, and the proceeds will be taxed as part of your estate when you die.

- You cannot be the trustee.

- You must establish the trust at least three years before your death. If the trust has not existed for at least three years when you die, the trust is disregarded for estate tax purposes and the proceeds are included in your taxable estate.

3. Charitable Remainder Trusts

With a charitable remainder trust, you make an irrevocable gift of property to a tax-exempt charity while you are alive. You are entitled to receive a pre-established income from the property during your life, and can achieve significant tax savings on both income and eventual estate tax. When you die, of course, the gift property must go to the charity.

For the wealthy, a charitable remainder trust can be a good way to make a donation and achieve some financial benefits. But if you don't want the property to go to a charity when you die, don't consider this kind of trust. The tax breaks will never equal the full worth of the gift property and the income you can earn from it.

For folks with more modest means, you can receive similar benefits, albeit of lesser dollar value, by making a gift to a "pooled" charitable trust, where your gift is combined with those of others.

Example: *Josie donates $10,000 to a pooled income charitable trust. The charity takes Josie's gift and combines it with other funds in the pool. Josie gets the following benefits:*

- *income for life (paid semi-annually) based on a set percentage of the charitable trust's net earnings,*
- *an income tax deduction of $10,000, less the present value of her right to receive the income for the trust for her life (this value is determined according to complicated IRS actuarial tables), and*
- *a $10,000 reduction in her taxable estate at death.*

4. Generation-Skipping Trusts

If you're downright rich, you might want to consider establishing a "generation-skipping" trust for the benefit of your grandchildren. This is a trust that pays only income to the middle generation—your children. When the children die, the trust principal is divided between the final beneficiaries, your grandchildren. (You can create this type of three-generation trust when the beneficiaries are other relations, or even non-relations, but in reality these trusts are almost always used for direct family generations.)

Special tax rules govern generation-skipping trusts. The property in the trust is included in your estate when you die. But the trust property is not included in the estates of any of the middle beneficiaries (the life beneficiaries). That means no additional tax is due when the children die and the grandchildren get the money.

The amount that can be passed this way is strictly limited to $1 million. This $1 million value is determined when you, the person who establishes the trust, die. Even if the trust property becomes worth $2, or $20 million, when the middle generation dies, no tax is due then.

If you leave property worth more than $1 million in a generation-skipping trust, it is subject to a stiff tax. Congress imposed the $1 million limit on these trusts to eliminate one of the estate tax dodges of the very rich. Before this limit, a multi-millionaire, or billionaire, could leave vast sums of money in generation-skipping trusts, effectively eliminating estate tax in every other generation.

Obviously, establishing this sort of trust makes sense only if your children have enough money to get along with only the interest, not the principal, of the trust property. My very limited experience hearing about the actual plans of rich people indicates you'll likely be at least in double-digit millions before you'll consider a generation- skipping trust.

D. Disclaiming Gifts

A disclaimer is not a trust, but it works something like one to lower overall estate tax. A disclaimer is a beneficiary's right to decline a gift or inheritance. There's no law that says that you must accept such a gift or that penalizes you if you don't.

With a well-prepared estate plan, a declined gift goes to the next in line for that property, normally the alternate beneficiary.

While a beneficiary has an independent right to disclaim a gift, this right is often expressly stated in a will or living trust, so the beneficiary clearly knows the disclaimer is O.K. with the person who left the property. Disclaimers are most frequently used to make a family's overall estate tax situation better.

Example: *Marie-Françoise, in her late 70s and quite well off, inherits $200,000 from her brother Martin's estate. The alternate beneficiary is Marie-Françoise's granddaughter Lola, an aspiring singer of classic French cabaret songs. Marie-Françoise doesn't need the money and if she accepts the gift, it will increase the size of her taxable estate. Martin's will expressly authorizes any beneficiary to disclaim a gift. Lola, whom Marie-Françoise loves, surely could use help. So, without worrying that she's not doing as Martin wanted, Marie-Françoise disclaims the gift, and it goes to Lola.* ■

CHAPTER 10

Property Control Trusts

You may want to, or believe you need to, control how your property is managed and distributed for an extended period of time after your death. For instance, if you're in a second marriage, you may want to ensure that property ultimately goes to your children from a former marriage, while also allowing your current spouse some benefits from the property. Or you may want to leave property to someone who, for one reason or another, can't manage it for himself, such as a disabled child.

The usual way to impose controls over your property after your death is by creating a trust. Here we'll look at how you can use different types of what I call "property control trusts" to achieve your goals. (A related concern, leaving property to a minor or young adult, is discussed in Chapter 3, Section C.)

Property Control Trusts Are Not a Do-it-Yourself Job. *You'll need to hire an attorney if you want to create any of the trusts discussed in this chapter.*

A. Marital Property Control Trusts for Second or Subsequent Marriages

In many second or subsequent marriages, one or both spouses may feel conflicted about estate planning. On one hand, a surviving spouse may well need use of or income from the deceased spouse's property, or may even need to spend some of that property to live comfortably. On the other hand, children from a former marriage may want a large portion of that property soon after their parent dies.

Even if children aren't insistent, a parent may want to help with their financial needs. Further, even if children are willing to wait for their inheritance until both spouses die, the children may still be understandably concerned that their inheritance be preserved, not consumed by a surviving spouse. These kinds of problems—which can be dicey at the best of times—become even more complicated if your spouse and children from a former marriage don't get along well.

You may be able to use a distinctive type of trust, which I call a "marital property control trust," to reconcile your desires for your spouse and children. With this kind of trust, you name your spouse as the life beneficiary for trust property. (As discussed earlier, a life beneficiary has defined rights to use trust property during his or her life, but no right to leave that property to anyone.) You name your children or other inheritors as the final beneficiaries, to receive all trust property after your spouse dies. If your spouse doesn't survive you, the trust property goes directly to your final beneficiaries when you die. If this all sounds familiar, that's because in many ways, this type of trust is similar to the AB trust discussed in Chapter 9. The biggest difference, discussed further below, is that the life beneficiary of a marital property control trust usually has more narrowly-defined, restricted rights to the trust property.

UNMARRIED COUPLES

This chapter talks in terms of subsequent marriages and surviving spouses, because most people who do this type of estate planning are married. But the principles apply equally to unmarried couples with children from previous relationships.

Example: *Tim and Margaurite are married; both are in their 50s. Tim has a son from his first marriage. Margaurite has two daughters from hers. The couple purchases a house for $380,000. Each contributes $70,000 toward the down payment, and mortgage payments will be shared equally. Each owns one-half of the house. When one spouse dies, each wants the other spouse to be able to live in the house for the remainder of his or her life. But after both have died, each wants his or her share of the house to go to the children of their first marriages. So Tim and Margaurite each create a marital property control trust. Each spouse's trust allows the surviving spouse full use of the house, but not the right to sell it. When the surviving spouse dies, half of the house goes to Tim's son, and the other half to Margaurite's two daughters.*

The key to a marital property control trust is that the rights of the surviving spouse to trust property are specifically limited and controlled as you define in the trust document. For instance, you may give your spouse the right to receive income from the trust, but no right whatsoever to spend trust principal. Or you can name someone else, not the surviving spouse, to be the trustee of the trust. This obviously reduces the surviving spouse's control over trust assets.

By placing sensible restrictions on your spouse's rights to trust property, you can feel confident that most or all of the trust principal will remain intact for your children. Marital property control trusts are, of course, no guarantee that family conflicts and tensions will be eliminated or even reduced. But they can provide legal control over your assets, and give you the comfort that you've done your best to provide for both your spouse and your children.

Figuring out exactly what restrictions you want to impose on the trust property can become complicated fast. Before finalizing a marital property control trust, you may need to work through many complexities. Here's where an experienced and empathetic lawyer can help, by raising the right questions—but not by dictating your answers. For example, to return to the house in Tim and Margaurite's trust:

- Who should be the trustee? The surviving spouse? Or is it better to have a child share that job with the surviving spouse? Or to have a child be the sole trustee?

- Can the surviving spouse rent the house to someone else? For any reason, or only if he or she cannot continue to occupy it for health reasons? What happens if the spouse no longer wants to live in the home? How long can the spouse leave the house vacant?

- If the house is rented, who decides what happens to the rental income? Can the surviving spouse use it to pay for his or her health needs? For any basic needs?

- How will you ensure that the house is properly maintained and all taxes and bills are paid?

- What reports and accountings of the trust property must the trustee give to the children?

Turning the answers to such questions into a binding, coherent legal document requires careful drafting—which is the major reason it will cost you a significant lawyer's fee to have a marital property control trust prepared.

Choosing the right trustee for a marital property control trust is vital. The trustee will have authority to manage the trust property and to make any authorized payments to the surviving spouse. Also, the trustee may have the responsibility of making sure that the surviving spouse is using the trust property as dictated by the trust. These duties can require diplomacy or tough decision-making.

Example: *Leticia, in her 70s, marries Ben, in his 60s. Leticia has been married twice before, and has one grown child from each marriage, a daughter, Lindsay, and a son, Kevin. Her estate consists of her house, worth $275,000 (all equity), plus savings and securities totaling $680,000. Ben owns much* less, about $40,000 in savings. He also receives a modest pension plus Social Security.

Ultimately, Leticia wants her property to pass equally to her two children. But if she dies before Ben, she doesn't want him thrown out on the street. She places her house and savings in a marital property control trust, giving Ben the right to live in the house and receive all income from the trust property during his life.

Kevin has made it clear he does not care for Ben. Lindsay and Ben have a tolerable relationship, though they aren't close. Ben tells Leticia that he wants to be trustee, because he'd prefer not to have his well-being ruled by one of her children. Kevin tells Leticia that he's sorry to say it, but he thinks Ben is improvident and could squander her estate. Leticia doubts this, but she doesn't want to take the risk. Kevin says he'd like to be the trustee. Although Kevin is a competent businessman, Leticia does not want to impose him on Ben. Lindsay, who's also levelheaded, tells Leticia she'd prefer not to be the trustee. But after considerable pondering, Leticia concludes that she has no one else she wants for the job. She persuades Lindsay that it will be best for all of them if she accepts the role of trustee, which she does. Then Leticia faces the delicate task of explaining her decision to Ben and Kevin, and trying to soothe any ruffled feelings.

The trust document gives Ben the right to remain in the house, with all its current furnishings, for his life. If he leaves it for more than four consecutive months, whether to move to some tropical paradise or a nursing home, the house and furnishings can be sold or rented if the trustee decides that's desirable. The trustee can either save that trust income as part of the trust principal, or spend it on Ben's needs.

Thus, Leticia leaves it up to Lindsay to decide what should happen to the house if Ben vacates it for more than four months. Leticia doesn't want to require that the house be turned over to her children in these circumstances. She just wants to protect her children, and not have the house stand empty for a long time. Leticia trusts Lindsay to make a wise decision if this matter comes up.

To stress the most vital point again, each marital property control trust involves the unique circumstances of the couple and final beneficiaries involved. There are no set rules dictating what's right. With this type of trust, you are inherently dealing with possible conflicts—the basic concern, after all, is that the surviving spouse's desires and interests may be very different from, or directly in conflict with, the desires and interests of the deceased spouse's children. Although you need a lawyer to help you work through issues about the trust, and draft the final version in clear language, the most important issues are practical, human ones: you must work out what's fair (as best you can) and decide who is best able to serve as successor trustee, overseeing your trust and carrying out your decisions. These concerns may be easy to state but, in real life, they can be quite difficult to resolve.

B. Special Needs Trusts for Disabled People

Parents or others who care about someone who has a serious physical or mental disability can face difficult estate planning questions. Understandably, they want to provide for the disabled person to whatever extent they can, for as long as that person lives. If the disabled person cannot manage property, the provider must create what's called a "special needs" trust. An attorney must draft the trust document carefully, so that the trustee has enough flexibility to deal with the beneficiary's medical or other special requirements.

There is no standard special needs trust that fits all circumstances. When setting up your trust, you must consider the beneficiary's particular needs and problems, as well as your own financial resources.

A primary concern with a special needs trust is making sure you select a trustee and one or more successor trustees who are willing and able to do the job. The trustee must be attentive to the disabled person's situation, discerning what is needed and providing for those needs to the fullest possible extent. The trustee must stay in close contact with the disabled person, so it is essential that the two get along. And finally, the trustee should have the savvy to deal with various institutions, from hospitals to banks to government agencies.

Another major concern when preparing a special needs trust is making sure that the trust's existence doesn't render the beneficiary ineligible for government assistance, such as Supplemental Security Income (SSI) or medical or educational aid. This fear is based in reality, because a disabled person who is the legal owner of any substantial amount of property usually must use up most or all of it before obtaining government assistance. In some circumstances, if a disabled person acquires property, the government may even demand reimbursement for past benefits.

Under U.S. Social Security Administration (SSA) guidelines, the property in a special needs trust doesn't affect eligibility for Social Security assistance if the beneficiary cannot:

- control the amount or frequency of trust payments, or
- revoke the trust and use the property.

In other words, the beneficiary must have no rights to demand and receive money from the trust income or principal. Nor can the beneficiary simply terminate the trust and take all the money in it. All control over payment of income or principal to the beneficiary must reside solely with the trustee. Normally, the trustee has power to spend money on behalf of the beneficiary for carefully defined needs that are not met by government aid.

More Information About Providing for a Disabled Person. *A good resource is* Planning for the Future: Providing a Meaningful Life for a Child With a Disability, *by Russell Grant and Joseph Fee (American Publishing Company).*

C. Education Trusts

If you want to create a structure to help pay for someone's college or other schooling, you can use an "education trust." These trusts are rarely set up by children's parents, who usually pay education costs directly, out of their own pockets. Commonly, grandparents or other older relatives create education trusts to aid young relations.

Creating an educational property control trust often involves complex issues including:

Deciding when the trust should become operational. If you are unlikely to live until a child begins college, you can arrange to have the trust begin your death. But if the child is older, near or at college age, you may want the trust to become operational right away. Before setting up a trust that begins during your life, you need to look into the gift tax consequences. The property you give to the trust will be a taxable gift. The gift tax exemption for educational costs won't apply, because that works only for money paid directly to an educational institution. (See Chapter 8, Section C.)

Deciding how each beneficiary qualifies for benefits. People take many different approaches to education, and you'll need to think about what limits, if any, you want to place on your trust beneficiary or beneficiaries. For example, must a beneficiary reach a certain education level—such as college or graduate school—to receive payments from the trust? If so, what qualifies as a college or graduate school? Your grandchild may discover another way to learn—for example, working with a well-known chef or dancer. Would the trustee have authority to approve the payment for this?

If you name multiple beneficiaries, deciding whether the trustee can pay unequal amounts for them. Your beneficiaries are likely to have different financial needs, depending on the educational paths they follow. For instance, if one child goes to a very expensive college and then a more expensive graduate school, her education may require a large portion of the total trust assets. Would your trustee be authorized to pay her tuition bills in full? Suppose some beneficiaries are much younger than others. Must the trustee retain a certain percentage of trust assets for each beneficiary?

Deciding what happens if new (potential) beneficiaries are born. If you're creating a trust for a group, such as all your grandchildren, do you want the trustee be able to make payments to new members of the group (new grandchildren) born after your death?

Deciding when the trust ends. You'll need to consider what should happen to any money left in the trust when no more beneficiaries are eligible for education payments. You might, for example, provide that all remaining money is divided equally between the beneficiaries. At another extreme, you could provide that the trustee decides how to distribute the money between the beneficiaries.

Facing these issues, you may wonder whether it's worth the effort to establish an education trust. Good question. Happily though, for quite a number of older, wealthier individuals, an education trust does make sense. With a good lawyer, you can create exactly the trust you want without great difficulty. Whatever work this involves will most likely be far outweighed by the satisfaction of knowing that you have secured the educational future (or, at least the costs of that future) for people you love.

D. Spendthrift Trusts

If you want to leave property to an adult who just can't handle money sensibly, a "spendthrift trust" is a good idea. The purpose of this type of trust is to restrict the beneficiary's ability to squander trust money. The beneficiary has no direct ownership rights over the trust property and no right to pledge trust principal, or future income expected from the trust, as security for a loan. Thus, the beneficiary's creditors cannot seize the trust property if he or she gets into financial hot water.

With a spendthrift trust, the trustee is always a different person than the beneficiary. When you design the trust, you give the trustee power to spend trust money to fit your specific situation and desires. Perhaps you want to allow your trustee to spend any amount she wants for the beneficiary's needs. Or, you might limit the trustee to paying only housing costs for the beneficiary. On the other hand, you may want the trustee to make payments directly to the beneficiary, if the trustee decides that's wise. Of course, once the trustee has turned money over to the beneficiary, the controls of the trust are gone for that money.

At the extreme, a spendthrift trust can give the trustee power to cut off all payments, temporarily or even permanently, to a beneficiary who becomes uncontrollably self-destructive. Income withheld may be accumulated in the trust or paid to another beneficiary named in the trust document.

As with the other property control trusts discussed in this chapter, if you want to set up a spendthrift trust, get thee to a good estate planning lawyer.

E. Flexible Trusts

You may not want to decide now precisely how your property should be distributed when you die. Instead, you may want to leave this decision in the hands of someone you trust. You can accomplish this by creating a "sprinkling trust," authorizing your trustee to spend trust money among, or for, several beneficiaries you've named. A sprinkling trust can work well if you have both complete confidence in your trustee, and a number of beneficiaries who may need varied payments over a long period of time.

The obvious difference between a sprinkling trust and all other property control trusts is that with the former you don't specify what property each beneficiary gets, or when. Rather, you leave money in a pot for two or more beneficiaries. (Indeed, a family pot trust for minors is one type of sprinkling trust. See Chapter 3, Section C.) The trustee alone decides which beneficiaries get payments, when, and how much. You can specify when the trust should end, and what happens to any money left in the trust, or you can leave these matters to the trustee. You may also impose certain limits on the trustee's discretion over trust property, such as requiring that each beneficiary receive at least 5% of trust income each year. ■

CHAPTER 11

Planning for Incapacity: Medical Care and Finances

As we grow older, we face the possibility of becoming mentally or physically incapacitated for some period of time, perhaps even for many years. Though it may be difficult to consider your own incapacity, a thorough estate plan should take this bleak possibility into account. You can plan ahead by preparing a few simple legal documents to ensure that your medical and financial wishes are carried out if you are unable to speak and act for yourself.

No matter what your age or the state of your health, preparing these documents—known as healthcare directives and a durable power of attorney for finances—should be part of your estate plan. Functionally, they work as a kind of insurance, becoming operational only if you do become unable to manage your own affairs. If don't put your wishes for these matters in writing and you become incapacitated, family members or close friends may have to file court proceedings to obtain legal authority to manage your affairs. These proceedings are time-consuming, public, sometimes embarrassing—and they usually rack up some lawyer's fees.

Planning for Long-Term Medical Care. *You may also want to plan for the possibility that you'll need long-term medical care. This is covered in* Beat the Nursing Home Trap: A Consumer's Guide to Assisted Living and Long-Term Care, *by Joseph Matthews (Nolo).*

A. Medical Decisions

In recent decades, the increasing use of life-sustaining medical technology has raised fears in many that our lives may be artificially prolonged against our wishes. The right to die with dignity, and without the tremendous agony and expense for both patient and family caused by prolonging lives artificially, has been confirmed by the U.S. Supreme Court, the federal government and every state legislature.

Writing down your wishes for medical care and appointing a trusted person to be sure those wishes are carried out can help alleviate fears, whether you worry about receiving unwanted medical treatment or you want healthcare providers to do all they can to prolong your life. It can also be a huge help to family members who might otherwise agonize about making medical decisions on your behalf.

1. Putting Your Wishes in Writing

Every state now has laws authorizing individuals to create simple documents setting out their wishes concerning life-prolonging medical care. There are two basic documents that allow you to do this, both grouped under the broad label "healthcare directives." You need to prepare both. First, you need a "declaration," a written statement you make directly to medical personnel which spells out the medical care you do or do not wish to receive if you become incapacitated. Your declaration functions as a contract with the treating doctor, who must either honor your wishes for medical care, or transfer you to another doctor or facility that will honor them.

Second, you'll want what's often called a "durable power of attorney for healthcare." In this document you appoint someone you trust to be your "attorney-in-fact" (sometimes called a "healthcare proxy") to see that your doctors and other healthcare providers give you the kind of medical care you wish to receive. In many states, you can also give your attorney-in-fact greater authority to make decisions about your medical care, including:

- hiring and firing medical personnel
- visiting you in the hospital or other facility even when other visiting is restricted

- having access to medical records and other personal information, and

- getting court authorization if it is required to obtain or withhold medical treatment if, for any reason, a hospital or doctor does not honor your healthcare directives.

A HEALTHCARE DIRECTIVE BY ANY OTHER NAME . . .

Depending upon the state, your healthcare documents may be called by one of several different names: Medical Directive, Directive to Physicians, Declaration Regarding Health Care, Designation of Health Care Surrogate, or Patient Advocate Designation. A healthcare declaration may also be called a "living will," but it bears no relation to the conventional will or living trust used to leave property at death.

Because your attorney-in-fact may have broad authority to direct your healthcare, it is crucial that you appoint someone who understands your wishes and will carry them out faithfully. Ideally, you will also name someone who:

- is likely to be present when decisions need to be made—most often, this means someone who lives nearby or who is willing to travel and spend time at your side during hospitalization

- would not easily be swayed or bullied by doctors or family members who disagree with your wishes, and

- is capable of grasping of your medical condition and any proposed medical treatments.

You should not appoint your doctor as your attorney-in-fact. In fact, laws in most states specifically forbid treating physicians from acting as a patient's attorney-in-fact. This eliminates the risk that they will have their own interests at heart and fail to act purely according to your wishes.

As long as you are of sound mind, you can change your healthcare directives in any way you wish, including appointing a new attorney-in-fact.

2. What You Can Cover in Your Healthcare Directives

As mentioned above, your healthcare declaration is the place to write out what you do and do not want in terms of medical care if you are unable to speak for yourself. You don't need to become a medical expert to complete your documents, but it will help you to become familiar with the kinds of medical procedures that are commonly administered to patients who are seriously ill. These include:

- blood and blood products
- cardiopulmonary resuscitation (CPR)
- diagnostic tests
- dialysis
- drugs
- respirators, and
- surgery.

You can discuss these procedures with your doctor or a patient representative of your health insurance plan, or you can turn to other resources, such as Nolo's *WillMaker* software, for more detailed information.

In addition to the medical procedures listed above, you may want to give some thought to the issues of pain medication, food and water. The laws of most states assume that people want relief from pain and discomfort and specifically exclude pain-relieving procedures from definitions of life-prolonging treatments that may be withheld. Some states also exclude food and water (commonly called nutrition and hydration) from their definitions of life-prolonging treatments. But there is some controversy about whether providing food and water, or drugs to make a person comfortable, will also have the effect of prolonging life.

If you feel adamant about not having your life prolonged, you may choose to direct that all food, water and pain relief be withheld, even if your treating physician thinks those procedures are necessary. Under the U.S. Constitution, you are allowed to leave these instructions even if your state's law is restrictive, and your doctors are bound to follow your wishes.

On the other hand, you may feel concerned about how much pain or discomfort you'll experience during a final illness. In this case, you may prefer to have your life prolonged rather than face the possibility that discomfort or pain will go untreated. Obviously, it's a very personal choice. You're free to leave the instructions that feel right for you.

WHEN YOUR HEALTHCARE DIRECTIVES TAKE EFFECT

Your healthcare directive becomes effective when three things happen:
- you are diagnosed as close to death from a terminal condition or permanently comatose—or, in a few sates, if you have one of a number of other serious conditions
- you cannot communicate your own wishes for your medical care—orally, in writing or through gestures, and
- the medical personnel attending you are notified of your written directions for your medical care.

In most instances, your directives become part of your medical record when you are admitted to a hospital or other care facility. But to ensure that your wishes will be followed if your need for care arises unexpectedly while you are out of your home state or country, it is best to give copies of your completed documents to several people, including your regular physician, your attorney-in-fact and another trusted friend.

---

3. Getting the Forms You Need

There are a number of ways to find the proper healthcare documents for your state; you don't need to consult a lawyer to obtain or prepare them. Here are some likely sources for forms and instructions:

- local senior centers
- local hospitals (ask to speak with the patient representative; by law, any hospital that receives federal funds must provide patients with appropriate forms for directing healthcare)
- your regular physician

- your state's medical association
- Nolo's *WillMaker* software (contains forms for all states except Louisiana, and thorough instructions to help you complete them)
- Choice in Dying, 1035 30th St. NW, Washington, DC 20007, 800-989-9455. (You can order the forms for a small fee, or you can download them for free from the organization's website at **http:www.choices.org**.)

4. Finalizing Your Healthcare Documents

Once you've filled in your healthcare directives, there are just a few steps you must take to finalize them. Every state requires that you sign your documents as a way of verifying that you understand them and that they contain your true wishes. If you are physically unable to sign them yourself, you can direct another person to sign them for you.

You must sign your documents, or have them signed for you, in the presence of witnesses or a notary public—sometimes both. (This depends on your state's law.) The purpose of this additional formality is so that there is at least one other person who can confirm that you were of sound mind and of legal age (at least 18) when you made the documents.

After your documents are complete, you should keep them where your attorney-in-fact can easily find them, if the need arises. Also, give copies to:

- your attorney-in-fact
- any physician with whom you now consult regularly
- the office of the hospital or other care facility in which you are likely to receive treatment
- any other people or institutions you think it's wise to inform of your medical intentions.

MAKING FINAL ARRANGEMENTS

When thinking about your estate plan, you might also consider what kind of body disposition and religious or other ceremonies you envision after your death. Leaving all this up to your survivors may result in confusion and pain at a time that is likely already difficult. Planning here can also help save some money. Without advance planning, funeral and related costs can be very expensive.

You can write out a statement of the type of ceremony you wish to have, including your desires regarding body disposition. In most all cases, your arrangements will be carried out as you specified. Do not include your statement in your will. Your statement must be readily accessible at your death by those who will carry out your wishes.

Obviously, the type of memorial you wish to have is a deeply personal matter. With body disposition, more and more people are reflecting on what they want to happen to their bodies when they die, and making choices that have emotional meaning for them and save their families needless expense. Broadly viewed, there are four choices:

- A traditional American funeral service, often including embalming of the body, conducted by a commercial funeral home, with subsequent cremation or burial
- A simple funeral service, without embalming, either with the help of a funeral or memorial society or by independent arrangement
- Donation of specific body organs to an organ bank. If organs are donated, the rest of the body is normally returned to those responsible for cremation or burial
- Donation of the entire body to medical school. This must be arranged beforehand. Usually, after the body is used for studies, it is then cremated.

For more information about making your final arrangements, you can contact the Funeral and Memorial Societies of America. Call 800-458-5563 or reach the organization online at www.funerals.org/famsa. You can also use Nolo's *WillMaker* (software for Windows or Macintosh) to create a final arrangements document, in addition to a valid will, healthcare directives and a durable power of attorney for finances.

B. Financial Decisions

A durable power of attorney for finances allows you to name someone you trust (called your attorney-in-fact) to handle your finances if you can't. Every state recognizes this type of document. If you become unable to manage your finances and you haven't prepared a durable power of attorney, your spouse, closest relatives or companion will have to ask a court for authority over at least some of your financial affairs. This procedure—called a conservatorship proceeding in most states— can be time-consuming and expensive. In contrast, preparing a durable power of attorney is simple and inexpensive—and if you do become incapacitated, the document will likely appear as a minor miracle to those closest to you.

1. Granting Authority to Your Attorney-in-Fact

Any power of attorney arrangement depends upon trust and under- standing between you and the person you appoint to handle your affairs. You can help make this relationship work by putting specific instruc- tions in your document regarding financial actions you do and do not wish the attorney-in-fact to take. Your attorney-in-fact has only the financial authority you grant him or her in the document. Normally, an attorney-in-fact has authority to handle all regular financial matters, such as depositing checks and paying bills. Beyond the basics of routine financial maintenance, it's up to you to decide what you want to autho- rize.

THE ATTORNEY-IN-FACT'S DUTIES

Commonly, people give an attorney-in-fact broad power over their finances. But you can give your attorney-in-fact as much or as little power as you wish. You may want to give your attorney-in-fact authority to do some or all of the following:

- use your assets to pay your everyday expenses and those of your family
- buy, sell, maintain, pay taxes on and mortgage real estate and other property
- collect benefits from Social Security, Medicare or other government programs or civil or military service
- invest your money in stocks, bonds and mutual funds
- handle transactions with banks and other financial institutions
- buy and sell insurance policies and annuities for you
- file and pay your taxes
- operate your small business
- claim or disclaim property you inherit or are otherwise entitled to
- represent you in court or hire someone to represent you, and
- manage your retirement accounts.

Whatever powers you give the attorney-in-fact, he or she must act in your best interests, keep accurate records, keep your property separate from his or hers (unless you specify otherwise in the power of attorney document) and avoid conflicts of interest.

While you may want to define and limit your attorney-in-fact's authority in some matters, you can't, obviously, foresee every financial concern which might arise. So it's vital that you choose someone you trust, and who has sound financial judgment, to be your attorney-in-fact. And while this doesn't have to be the same person as you choose as attorney-in-fact for your healthcare directives, it's sensible to name the same person for both roles unless you strongly believe someone else should handle your money. If you do name different people for these two jobs, be sure they can work well together.

As with healthcare directives, you can change the attorney-in-fact or any other provision of your durable power of attorney for finances any time, as long as you are of sound mind.

How to Find the Forms You Need. *You can use Nolo's* WillMaker *software to prepare a durable power of attorney for finances that is valid in your state. You can also obtain the necessary forms and instructions from* The Financial Power of Attorney Workbook, *by Shae Irving (Nolo).*

2. When Your Durable Power of Attorney for Finances Takes Effect

There are two kinds of durable powers of attorney for finances: those that take effect immediately, and those that don't become effective unless a doctor (or two, if you wish) certifies that you are incapacitated. Which to choose depends, in part, on when you want your attorney-in-fact to begin handling tasks for you.

If you want someone to take over some or all of your financial tasks now, you should make your document effective as soon as you sign it. Then, your attorney-in-fact can begin helping you with your finances right away—and can continue to do so if you later become incapacitated.

On the other hand, you may feel strongly that your attorney-in-fact should not take over unless and until you are incapacitated. In this case, you have two options. If you trust your attorney-in-fact to use his or her authority only when it's absolutely necessary, you can go ahead and make your durable power of attorney effective immediately. Legally, your attorney-in-fact will then have the authority to act on your behalf—but, according to your wishes, won't do so unless he or she ever decides that you can't handle your affairs yourself.

If you're uncomfortable making a document that's effective immediately, you can make what's known as a "springing" power of attorney. It doesn't take effect until a physician examines you and declares, in writing, that you can't manage your finances.

There are some real inconveniences involved in creating a springing power of attorney. First, your attorney-in-fact will have to go through the potentially time-consuming and complicated process of getting the doctors' statements. And second, though it's not too likely, some people and institutions may be reluctant to accept a springing power of attorney, even after the your attorney-in fact has obtained the necessary doctors' statements and your document is perfectly legal. A bank, for example, might question whether you have, in fact, become incapacitated. These hassles could delay your attorney-in-fact and disrupt the handling of your finances.

If you truly trust your attorney-in-fact (and you should), you may find that it makes more sense to create a document that's effective immediately and then make clear to your attorney-in-fact when he or she should take action under the document. Ultimately, of course, the decision is yours—and you should choose the option that feels most comfortable to you.

3. Finalizing Your Durable Power of Attorney for Finances

After you've completed your durable power of attorney for finances, you must observe certain formalities to make it legal. But these requirements aren't difficult to meet.

You must sign your durable power of attorney in the presence of a notary public for your state. In some states, notarization is required by law to make the durable power of attorney valid. But even where law doesn't require it, custom does. A durable power of attorney that is not notarized may not be accepted by people your attorney-in-fact needs to deal with. A handful of states also require you to sign your document in front of witnesses. Witnesses must be mentally competent adults, and your attorney-in-fact may not be a witness. Some states impose additional witness requirements as well.

Finally, if your document grants power over real estate, you must put a copy of your document on file in the land records office of any counties where you own real estate. This process is called "recording," or "registration" in some states. In just two states, North Carolina and South Carolina, you must record your durable power of attorney for it to be durable—that is, for it to remain in effect if you become incapacitated.

WHAT TO DO WITH THE SIGNED DOCUMENT

If your power of attorney is effective immediately, give the original, signed and notarized document to the attorney-in-fact. He or she will need it as proof of authority to act on your behalf.

If the durable power of attorney won't become effective unless you become incapacitated (a springing durable power of attorney), keep the notarized, signed original yourself. Store it in a safe, convenient place that the attorney-in-fact can reach quickly, if necessary. Your attorney-in-fact will need the original document to carry out your wishes.

You may also wish to give copies of your durable power of attorney to the people and institutions your attorney in fact will need to deal with—banks or government offices, for example. If the document is already in their records, it may eliminate hassles for your attorney-in-fact later. If you're making a springing durable power of attorney, however, it may seem premature to contact people and institutions about a document that may never go into effect. It's up to you.

Lawyers

Must you hire an attorney to do your estate planning competently? You surely know my answer by now. As I've stated many times in this book, with good self-help materials, many people can handle all their own estate planning work. Others will decide that they do need an attorney, for one or more sensible reasons. Then the concern becomes finding a good lawyer, for a fair fee.

A. Will You Need a Lawyer?

Every estate plan involves some legal documents—at least a will, usually a living trust and durable powers of attorney, and perhaps other papers. Ask yourself whether you're willing to do some or all of the legal work for your estate planning. If you answer no, and you know that you will never get around to learning how to prepare legal documents even if it will save you money, then you'll need to hire a lawyer. (There's nothing inherently wrong with this approach, of course; it's your money and your time, and it's certainly not my job to tell you how to apportion the two.)

On the other hand, if you are willing to do your own legal work, and you have a relatively simple estate plan, you should be able to prepare the documents you want without hiring a lawyer. The key is that phrase "relatively simple." Roughly, it means having a straightforward beneficiary plan and an estate that won't be liable for estate tax, except perhaps for property that can shielded from tax by an AB trust.

You may, understandably, remain doubtful about preparing your own documents. Perhaps you feel that you can understand the basic concepts, but are dubious about actually preparing the papers. Indeed, many people are so intimidated by estate planning that they fear that without a lawyer, they'll do something wrong, and that their property won't be distributed as they wish.

The fact that so many people worry that estate planning requires a lawyer surely shows how fear-ridden our legal system has become. To dispel some of this fear, let's look realistically at what's involved when you prepare a will or living trust. The core transaction is generally quite simple: people just want to leave their property to who they want to get it after they die. What's inherently complicated about that? Nothing. Indeed, as I've already noted, many people can state in a sentence or two what they want.

Example 1: *I want all my property to go to my wife Yvonne Kamner, or if she dies before I do, to be divided equally between my three children.*

Example 2: *I want my house and all my other property to go to my sister Charlotte O'Malley. If she dies before me I want my property sold and the money divided equally between The Red Cross, The Audubon Society and CARE.*

Example 3: *I want half the value of my property to go my husband Bill Tarver and the other half divided equally between my children Christopher Reilly and Mona Reilly Jamison.*

Do not believe the lawyers, or estate planning books, that tell you it's crazy to do-it-yourself. Preparing a basic will, living trust or durable power of attorney is not like creating a new computer or designing a house. While very wealthy people may benefit from the services of a lawyer, you're probably not looking for cutting-edge estate planning maneuvers, and can safely prepare your own documents.

Let me stress one final point about deciding whether you need a lawyer. Your estate plan should express your intentions—and no one else can decide for you what those intentions are. Sometimes when people think, or fear, that they need a lawyer, what they are really doing is longing for an authority figure (or believing one is required) to tell them what to do. But only you can decide who should get your property, and how and when they should get it. If you want to talk things over with someone you trust, that's fine and good. However, at most, an estate planning expert should be your legal technician and advisor, not your mentor.

B. Using Lawyers

Lawyers are costly. Estate planning fees usually range from $150 to $400 per hour. But if your situation is complex and you want professional help, a good lawyer can be well worth the cost. Here's some thoughts on finding a lawyer you'll like.

1. Hiring a Lawyer to Review Your Estate Planning Documents

Hiring a lawyer solely to review the legal documents you create yourself may sound like a good idea. It shouldn't cost much, and it seems to offer a comforting security. Sadly, though, it may be difficult or even impossible to find a lawyer who will accept the job.

While this is unfortunate, I'm not willing to excoriate lawyers who won't review do-it-yourself estate planning documents. From their point of view, they are being asked to accept what might turn into a significant responsibility for what they regard as inadequate compensation, given their usual fees. Any prudent lawyer sees every client as a potential occasion for a malpractice claim, or at least, serious later hassles—for example, a phone call four years down the line that begins, "I talked to you about my living trust, and now . . . ." Most experienced lawyers want to avoid this kind of risk. Also, many lawyers feel that if they're only reviewing someone else's work, they simply don't get deeply enough into a situation to be sure of their opinions. Then there's the truth that beyond the few formal, legal requirements and technical exceptions, there's no one right way to prepare, say, a will or a living trust. Unfortunately, some lawyers think this means that if you haven't prepared your documents their way, you've done it wrong.

If you feel that you really need an attorney to review your documents, all I can suggest is that you keep trying to find a sympathetic lawyer—perseverance may pay off. Also be prepared to pay enough to make the lawyer feel adequately compensated for the work and assumption of responsibility.

2. Finding a Lawyer

If you want to hire a lawyer but don't know one, how do you find a lawyer who is trustworthy, competent and charges fairly? A few words of advice may be helpful.

a. What Type of Lawyer Do You Need?

First, decide what type of lawyer you need. Estate planning lawyers fall into three categories:

- general practice lawyers
- estate planning specialists, and
- highly specialized lawyers working in one very difficult aspect of estate planning.

Which type is right for you depends on your estate planning concerns and needs.

- **General Practice Lawyers.** General practice lawyers handle all sorts of cases; they don't specialize in estate planning. If your needs are basic, such as a garden-variety living trust or will, or researching some aspect of your state's laws, a competent attorney in general practice should be able to do a good job at a lower cost than more specialized attorneys.

- **Estate Planning Specialists.** For any type of sophisticated estate planning work, ranging from estate-tax savings to property control trusts, you need to see a specialist. To do a good job with higher-end estate planning, a lawyer needs to be absolutely up-to-date on estate tax law and regulations, the rules governing ongoing trusts and numerous other matters. Most general practice lawyers are simply not sufficiently educated in this field. An expert may charge relatively high fees—but a good expert is well worth it. Also, it's worth noting that if you need estate tax planning, you (or you and your spouse together) can surely afford it.

- **Highly Specialized Lawyers.** Some lawyers specialize in a particularly difficult aspect of estate law, such as multinational estate planning or preparing QDOT trusts for property left to non-citizen spouses. Another example is the preparation of "special needs" trusts for disabled people. To do a good job here, a lawyer must be current on complex federal and state regulations regarding trust property and eligibility for government benefits. Even most estate planning experts don't have sufficient expertise for this.

b. How to Look for a Lawyer

After you decide what type of lawyer you need, it's time to look for the individual who can best help you. You should actually enjoy working with your estate planning lawyer. Ideally, you'll find one with whom you have personal rapport and who treats you as an equal. From a lawyer's point of view (at least this lawyer) one of the best things about estate planning work is that you are not seeing people in crisis, and not making money off their misery, as so much lawyering does (accident victims, divorces, accused criminals, anyone in litigation). With good estate planning, everybody wins, except probate lawyers and the taxman.

When looking for a good lawyer, especially an estate planning expert, personal routes are the traditional, and probably best, method. If a relative or friend who has good business and financial sense knows an estate planning lawyer she recommends, chances are you'll like him too. Failing this, check with people you know in any political or social organization with which you're involved, especially those with a large number of members over age 40. Assuming they themselves are savvy, they may well be able to point you to a competent lawyer who handles estate planning matters and whose attitudes are similar to yours.

Another good approach is to ask for help from a lawyer you know personally and think well of, no matter what area she works in. Very likely she can refer you to someone trustworthy who is an estate planning expert.

Yet another possibility is to check with people you respect who own their own small businesses. Almost anyone running a small business has a relationship with a lawyer, and chances are they've found one they like. Again, this lawyer will probably not be an estate planning expert, but he'll likely know one, or several.

If you need a lawyer with highly specialized skills, she may be difficult to find. In some states, such as California, state bar associations certify lawyers as expert estate planners, but even this is no guarantee they are competent in one of the very specialized areas of estate planning. You simply have to seek until you find a lawyer you trust who has the expertise you need.

And finally, a warning: be prudent with lawyer referral services, often run by county bar associations, which will give you the names of some attorneys who practice in your geographic area. The referral service usually provides only minimal screening for the attorneys listed, which means those who participate may not be the most experienced or competent. It may be possible to find a skilled attorney willing to work for a reasonable fee following this approach, but be sure to ask the attorney about her credentials and experience.

Personally evaluate any lawyer you've been referred to before you agree to have him handle your estate plan. Don't hesitate to question the lawyer, no matter how expert he is considered to be.

No matter how charming and sympathetic your lawyer, be sure you've settled your fee arrangement—in writing—at the start of your relationship. In addition to the amount charged per hour, it's also prudent to get an estimate of how many hours your lawyer expects to put in on your matter.

C. Doing Your Own Research

Instead of hiring a lawyer, you may decide to do your own legal research. Of course, legal research isn't for everyone. You need energy, patience and the ability and desire to enter a new mental world. If you're intrepid, however, you'll probably save money on attorney's fees, and, hopefully, feel satisfied that you've acquired at least some sense of mastery over an area of law.

The best book explaining how to do your own legal work is *Legal Research: How to Find and Understand the Law*, by Steve Elias and Susan Levinkind (Nolo). It shows you, step-by-step, how to find answers in the law library and is, as far as I know, the only legal research book written specifically for non-professionals.

⚠️ **Don't Get in Too Deep.** *While I applaud people who tackle their own legal research, I'll admit I rarely found legal research to be much fun. And if you're investigating complicated legal issues, it can trip you up. You must be especially careful when investigating estate tax matters. The Internal Revenue Code is abstruse, dense and potentially treacherous. If you want an estate tax saving trust that may save your inheritors tens or hundred of thousands of dollars, it's far wiser to hire an expert than to try to become one yourself.*

Another way to approach legal research is to use a computer. If you want information about current estate planning issues, such as a recent court decision or a new statute, you'll probably be able to find it somewhere on the World Wide Web. Many public libraries now offer online access, if you're not connected at home or work.

The Nolo.com website offers extensive materials on estate planning. You can find us at **www.nolo.com**. ■

Finalizing Your Estate Plan

Once you've decided on your estate plan and completed the documents you want, are you all done? Basically, yes—except (ah, the eternal "except")—except for storing your documents and making any subsequent changes you decide are necessary. Here's a commonsense approach to storing your documents, and some basic rules about when and how to make changes to your plans.

A. Storing Your Estate Planning Documents

Finishing your estate plan means that you have created some important documents: a will, probably a living trust, healthcare directives, a durable power of attorney for finances, and possibly others, ranging from pay-on-death-account records to revised business ownership papers. Obviously, you need to keep all these documents in a safe place, where you and your executor/successor trustee and attorney-in-fact can readily find them. This should be easy to accomplish. Any secure place can be used for storage: a safe in your house or office, or a drawer in your home desk or file cabinet. Using a bank safe-deposit box is probably overcautious, and possibly burdensome. Your executor may not have access to the box after your death, and there's a chance the box will be sealed if your estate owes state death tax. In any case, the worry with estate planning documents isn't that they'll be stolen (they have no street value, after all) but that they'll be lost. Using a secure place in your home or office, one that your executor/successor trustee and attorney-in-fact know about, should solve this worry.

You can make and distribute as many copies of your documents as you want. You may choose to give copies to beneficiaries and other concerned people so they know the details of your estate plan. For example, some people give a copy of their living trust to each beneficiary. You may also want to give copies of your healthcare directives to your attorney-in-fact, primary care physician and local hospital. And it's often desirable to give copies of a durable power of attorney for finances to your attorney-in-fact and any institutions he or she will be dealing with. Finally, you may need copies of your estate planning documents for other reasons, such as demonstrating to a financial institution that you do have a valid living trust.

While using copies is often helpful, making duplicate originals is always a bad idea. A duplicate original is a document prepared with the same formality as the first original. For example, with a duplicate original will, the document is signed and dated by the willmaker and witnesses, just as the first original was. Duplicate originals are a bad idea because each original, whether first or duplicate, is a separate, legally-valid document. If you later decide to amend or revoke the document, you must do so with every duplicate original. At best, this will be a hassle. At worst, you risk creating conflicting documents, if you fail to amend or revoke any duplicate original.

B. Revising Your Estate Plan

Unlike chic contemporary painting or haute couture clothes, estate plans are not designed for frequent change. Indeed, many people never need to revise or amend their plan. However, major life events frequently call for estate planning changes. If any of the following events occur, you should review your plan:

You get married. In the great majority of states, if you don't update your will, your new spouse will have the right under state law to inherit a certain portion of your estate. (See Chapter 2, Section A.)

You have or adopt a child. The rule here is similar to that for marriage. (See Chapter 2, Section D.)

You get divorced. In some states, a divorce ends a former spouse's right to inherit under a will. In other states, it doesn't. Also, property left to a divorced spouse using devices other than a will may not be affected by a divorce. If you've made a durable power of attorney for finances and named your former spouse as attorney-in-fact, divorce may terminate his or her authority, depending on your state.

A beneficiary dies. You'll want to revise your plan to arrange for alternate disposition of the affected property.

You want to put someone else in charge of your plans. For various reasons, you may want to change the executor of your will, or the successor trustee of your living trust. Or you may want to name a different attorney-in-fact under your durable power of attorney for healthcare or finances. You may also want to change the personal or property guardian you have named for your minor children or, if you have established a children's trust or pot trust, the person you have named as trustee, or custodian for a gift under the UTMA.

Your financial or property situation changes significantly. This includes the sale or gift of any property you've specifically left to a named beneficiary.

You move to a new state. Your will and living trust remain legal and valid if you move to a different state after establishing them. However, there are a couple of reasons to check out some of your new state's estate planning laws. First, the new state might require a different form for healthcare documents or have different rules about finalizing a durable power of attorney for finances. Your old documents will most likely be honored in the new state, but your attorney(s)-in-fact will have an easier time if all your documents are made under the laws of your new home.

Second, if you are married, and move from a common law state to a community property state or vice versa, you should learn how the laws of your new state affect marital property ownership. (To learn which states are community property states, see the list in Chapter 2, Section A.)

If you do decide to change your estate plan, you must usually decide whether you need, or want, to create entirely new documents or simply modify your existing ones. Generally, the more significant the changes, the more desirable it is to prepare a brand new document. Also, if you prepared your original document using a computer, it may actually be easier to prepare a new document than to amend your old one.

If you do create a new document, you must formally revoke your old one. For example, most wills state near the beginning "I revoke all previous wills I have made," just to be sure any earlier will has been invalidated. You should also physically destroy—tear up—your old document. If you can round up any copies of your old document, it's sensible to destroy them, too. But you don't need to get hung up over this. As long as it is clear that your revoked the original of your old document, a copy of that old document cannot be used to invalidate your new document.

If you want to amend an existing document, what to do depends on the type of document at hand. An existing will can be amended by a formal document called a "codicil," a sort of legal "P.S." to the will. It must be executed with the formalities of a will, including using two witnesses.

A living trust can be revised fairly easily by a typed amendment. You must sign and date the amendment and have it notarized.

Other estate planning devices can also be easily changed. For instance, you can amend or revoke a pay-on-death account at any time. You can change a beneficiary simply by deleting the old one and entering a new one on the appropriate form. Indeed, as long as you are competent, you can change any part of your plan, except (there it is again) for certain irrevocable tax saving trusts, such as a life insurance trust or a charitable remainder trust. ■

INDEX

CATALOG

...more from nolo.com

		PRICE	CODE

BUSINESS

		PRICE	CODE
⊙	The CA Nonprofit Corp Kit (Binder w/CD-ROM)	$39.95	CNP
▣	Consultant & Independent Contractor Agreements (Book w/Disk—PC)	$24.95	CICA
▣	The Corporate Minutes Book (Book w/Disk—PC)	$69.95	CORMI
	The Employer's Legal Handbook	$31.95	EMPL
▣	Form Your Own Limited Liability Company (Book w/Disk—PC)	$34.95	LIAB
▣	Hiring Independent Contractors: The Employer's Legal Guide (Book w/Disk—PC)	$29.95	HICI
▣	How to Create a Buy-Sell Agreement and Control the Destiny of your Small Business (Book w/Disk—PC)	$49.95	BSAG
▣	How to Form a California Professional Corporation (Book w/Disk—PC)	$49.95	PROF
▣	How to Form a Nonprofit Corporation (Book w/Disk —PC)—National Edition	$39.95	NNP
	How to Form a Nonprofit Corporation in California	$34.95	NON
▣	How to Form Your Own California Corporation (Binder w/Disk—PC	$39.95	CACI
▣	How to Form Your Own California Corporation (Book w/Disk—PC)	$34.95	CCOR
▣	How to Form Your Own Florida Corporation (Book w/Disk—PC)	$39.95	FLCO
▣	How to Form Your Own New York Corporation (Book w/Disk—PC)	$39.95	NYCO
▣	How to Form Your Own Texas Corporation (Book w/Disk—PC)	$39.95	TCOR
	How to Write a Business Plan	$24.95	SBS
	The Independent Paralegal's Handbook	$29.95	PARA
	Legal Guide for Starting & Running a Small Business, Vol. 1	$24.95	RUNS
▣	Legal Guide for Starting & Running a Small Business, Vol. 2: Legal Forms (Book w/Disk—PC)	$29.95	RUNS2
	Marketing Without Advertising	$19.00	MWAD
▣	Music Law (Book w/Disk—PC)	$29.95	ML

▣   Book with disk
⊙   Book with CD-ROM

⌨ Book with disk

◉ Book with CD-ROM

	PRICE	CODE
The Guardianship Book (California Edition)	$39.95	GB
How to Adopt Your Stepchild in California	$34.95	ADOP
How to Raise or Lower Child Support in California (Quick & Legal Series)	$19.95	CHLD
A Legal Guide for Lesbian and Gay Couples	$25.95	LG
The Living Together Kit	$29.95	LTK
Nolo's Pocket Guide to Family Law	$14.95	FLD
Using Divorce Mediation: Save Your Money & Your Sanity	$21.95	UDMD

GOING TO COURT

	PRICE	CODE
Beta Your Ticket: Go To Court and Win! (National Edition)	$19.95	BEYT
Collect Your Court Judgment (California Edition)	$29.95	JUDG
The Criminal Law Handbook: Know Your Rights, Survive the System	$24.95	KYR
Everybody's Guide to Small Claims Court (National Edition)	$18.95	NSCC
Everybody's Guide to Small Claims Court in California	$18.95	CSCC
Fight Your Ticket ... and Win! (California Edition)	$19.95	FYT
How to Change Your Name in California	$34.95	NAME
How to Mediate Your Dispute	$18.95	MEDI
How to Seal Your Juvenile & Criminal Records (California Edition)	$24.95	CRIM
How to Sue For Up to $25,000...and Win!	$29.95	MUNI
Mad at Your Lawyer	$21.95	MAD
Represent Yourself in Court: How to Prepare & Try a Winning Case	$29.95	RYC

HOMEOWNERS, LANDLORDS & TENANTS

		PRICE	CODE
▣	Contractors' and Homeowners' Guide to Mechanics' Liens (Book w/Disk—PC)	$39.95	MIEN
	The Deeds Book (California Edition)	$24.95	DEED
	Dog Law	$14.95	DOG
▣	Every Landlord's Legal Guide (National Edition, Book w/Disk—PC)	$34.95	ELLI
	Every Tenant's Legal Guide	$26.95	EVTEN
	For Sale by Owner in California	$24.95	FSBO
	How to Buy a House in California	$24.95	BHCA
	The Landlord's Law Book, Vol. 1: Rights & Responsibilities (California Edition)	$34.95	LBRT
	The Landlord's Law Book, Vol. 2: Evictions (California Edition)	$34.95	LBEV
	Leases & Rental Agreements (Quick & Legal Series)	$18.95	LEAR
	Neighbor Law: Fences, Trees, Boundaries & Noise	$17.95	NEI

▣ Book with disk
◉ Book with CD-ROM

	PRICE	CODE
Renters' Rights (National Edition—Quick & Legal Series))	$15.95	RENT
Stop Foreclosure Now in California	$29.95	CLOS
Tenants' Rights (California Edition)	$21.95	CTEN

HUMOR

	PRICE	CODE
29 Reasons Not to Go to Law School	$9.95	29R
Poetic Justice	$9.95	PJ

IMMIGRATION

	PRICE	CODE
How to Get a Green Card: Legal Ways to Stay in the U.S.A.	$24.95	GRN
U.S. Immigration Made Easy	$44.95	IMEZ

MONEY MATTERS

	PRICE	CODE
⊡ 101 Law Forms for Personal Use (Quick & Legal Series, Book w/disk—PC)	$24.95	SPOT
Bankruptcy: Is It the Right Solution to Your Debt Problems? (Quick & Legal Series)	$15.95	BRS
Chapter 13 Bankruptcy: Repay Your Debts	$29.95	CH13
Credit Repair (Quick & Legal Series)	$15.95	CREP
⊡ The Financial Power of Attorney Workbook (Book w/disk—PC)	$24.95	FINPOA
How to File for Chapter 7 Bankruptcy	$26.95	HFB
IRAs, 401(k)s & Other Retirement Plans: Taking Your Money Out	$21.95	RET
Money Troubles: Legal Strategies to Cope With Your Debts	$19.95	MT
Nolo's Law Form Kit: Personal Bankruptcy	$16.95	KBNK
Stand Up to the IRS	$24.95	SIRS
Take Control of Your Student Loans	$19.95	SLOAN

PATENTS AND COPYRIGHTS

	PRICE	CODE
⊡ The Copyright Handbook: How to Protect and Use Written Works (Book w/disk—PC)	$29.95	COHA
Copyright Your Software	$24.95	CYS
How to Make Patent Drawings Yourself	$29.95	DRAW
The Inventor's Notebook	$19.95	INOT
⊡ License Your Invention (Book w/Disk—PC)	$39.95	LICE
Patent, Copyright & Trademark	$24.95	PCTM
Patent It Yourself	$46.95	PAT

⊡ Book with disk

⊙ Book with CD-ROM

	PRICE	CODE
Patent Searching Made Easy	$24.95	PATSE
Software Development: A Legal Guide (Book with CD-ROM)	$44.95	SFT

RESEARCH & REFERENCE

		PRICE	CODE
⊙	Government on the Net (Book w/CD-ROM—Windows/Macintosh)	$39.95	GONE
⊙	Law on the Net (Book w/CD-ROM—Windows/Macintosh)	$39.95	LAWN
	Legal Research: How to Find & Understand the Law	$24.95	LRES
	Legal Research Made Easy (Video)	$89.95	LRME
⊙	Legal Research Online & in the Library (Book w/CD-ROM—Windows/Macintosh)	$39.95	LRO

SENIORS

	PRICE	CODE
Beat the Nursing Home Trap	$21.95	ELD
The Conservatorship Book (California Edition)	$44.95	CNSV
Social Security, Medicare & Pensions	$21.95	SOA

SOFTWARE

Call or check our website at www.nolo.com for special discounts on Software!

		PRICE	CODE
⊙	LeaseWriter CD—Windows/Macintosh	$99.95	LWD1
⊙	Living Trust Maker CD—Windows/Macintosh	$79.95	LTD2
⊙	Small Business Legal Pro 3 CD—Windows/Macintosh	$79.95	SBCD3
⊙	Personal RecordKeeper 5.0 CD—Windows/Macintosh	$59.95	RKD5
⊙	Patent It Yourself CD—Windows	$229.95	PPC12
⊙	WillMaker 7.0 CD—Windows/Macintosh	$69.95	WMD7

Special Upgrade Offer

Get 35% off the latest edition off your Nolo book

It's important to have the most current legal information. Because laws and legal procedures change often, we update our books regularly. To help keep you up-to-date we are extending this special upgrade offer. Cut out and mail the title portion of the cover of your old Nolo book and we'll give you 35% off the retail price of the NEW EDITION of that book when you purchase directly from us. For more information call us at 1-800-992-6656. This offer is to individuals only.

▣ Book with disk
⊙ Book with CD-ROM

ORDER FORM

Code	Quantity	Title	Unit price	Total
		Subtotal		
		California residents add Sales Tax		
		Basic Shipping ($3.95)		
		UPS RUSH delivery $8.00–any size order*		
		TOTAL		

Name

Address

(UPS to street address, Priority Mail to P.O. boxes)   * Delivered in 3 business days from receipt of S.F. Bay Area use regular shipping. order.

FOR FASTER SERVICE, USE YOUR CREDIT CARD & OUR TOLL-FREE NUMBERS

Order 24 hours a day   1-800-992-6656
Fax your order   1-800-645-0895
Online   www.nolo.com

METHOD OF PAYMENT

☐ Check enclosed
☐ VISA   ☐ MasterCard   ☐ Discover Card   ☐ American Express

Account #   Expiration Date

Authorizing Signature

Daytime Phone

PRICES SUBJECT TO CHANGE.

VISIT OUR STORE   VISIT US ONLINE

You'll find our complete line of books and software, all at a discount.

950 Parker Street
Berkeley, CA 94710
1-510-704-2248

on the Internet
www.nolo.com

NOLO.COM 950 PARKER ST., BERKELEY, CA 94710

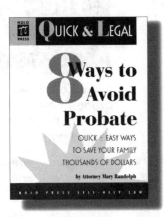
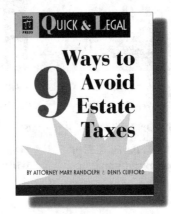

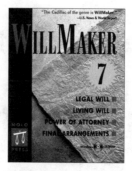
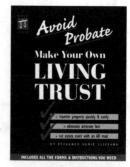
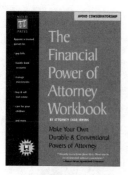
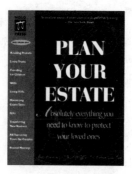

Take 2 minutes & Give us your 2 cents

Your comments make a big difference in the development and revision of Nolo books and software. Please take a few minutes and register your Nolo product—and your comments—with us. Not only will your input make a difference, you'll receive special offers available only to registered owners of Nolo products on our newest books and software. Register now by:

PHONE
1-800-992-6656

FAX
1-800-645-0895

EMAIL
cs@nolo.com

or **MAIL** us
this registration card

REMEMBER:
Little publishers have big ears. We really listen to you.

fold here

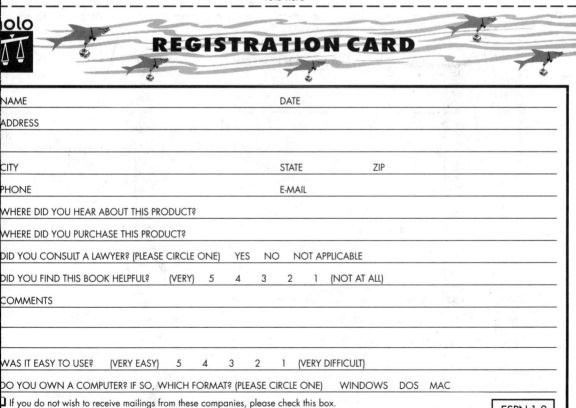

REGISTRATION CARD

NAME		DATE	
ADDRESS			
CITY		STATE	ZIP
PHONE		E-MAIL	

WHERE DID YOU HEAR ABOUT THIS PRODUCT?

WHERE DID YOU PURCHASE THIS PRODUCT?

DID YOU CONSULT A LAWYER? (PLEASE CIRCLE ONE)   YES   NO   NOT APPLICABLE

DID YOU FIND THIS BOOK HELPFUL?   (VERY)   5   4   3   2   1   (NOT AT ALL)

COMMENTS

WAS IT EASY TO USE?   (VERY EASY)   5   4   3   2   1   (VERY DIFFICULT)

DO YOU OWN A COMPUTER? IF SO, WHICH FORMAT? (PLEASE CIRCLE ONE)   WINDOWS   DOS   MAC

☐ If you do not wish to receive mailings from these companies, please check this box.
☐ You can quote me in future Nolo Press promotional materials. Daytime phone number _____

ESPN 1.0

NOLO IN THE NEWS

"Nolo helps lay people perform legal tasks without the aid—or fees—of lawyers."

—USA TODAY

Nolo books are ..."written in plain language, free of legal mumbo jumbo, and spiced with witty personal observations."

—ASSOCIATED PRESS

"...Nolo publications...guide people simply through the how, when, where and why of law."

—WASHINGTON POST

"Increasingly, people who are not lawyers are performing tasks usually regarded as legal work... And consumers, using books like Nolo's, do routine legal work themselves."

—NEW YORK TIMES

"...All of [Nolo's] books are easy-to-understand, are updated regularly, provide pull-out forms...and are often quite moving in their sense of compassion for the struggles of the lay reader."

—SAN FRANCISCO CHRONICLE

fold here

- -

nolo.com
950 Parker Street
Berkeley, CA 94710-9867

Attn: | **ESPN 1.0** |